The benefits of
subsidized housing programs

The benefits of subsidized housing programs

An intertemporal approach

CLAIRE HOLTON HAMMOND
Wake Forest University

*The right of the
University of Cambridge
to print and sell
all manner of books
was granted by
Henry VIII in 1534.
The University has printed
and published continuously
since 1584.*

CAMBRIDGE UNIVERSITY PRESS

Cambridge
New York New Rochelle
Melbourne Sydney

CAMBRIDGE UNIVERSITY PRESS
Cambridge, New York, Melbourne, Madrid, Cape Town, Singapore, São Paulo

Cambridge University Press
The Edinburgh Building, Cambridge CB2 8RU, UK

Published in the United States of America by Cambridge University Press, New York

www.cambridge.org
Information on this title: www.cambridge.org/9780521327527

First published 1987
This digitally printed version 2008

A catalogue record for this publication is available from the British Library

Library of Congress Cataloguing in Publication data
Hammond, Claire Holton, 1951–
The benefits of subsidized housing programs.
Bibliography: p.
Includes index.
1. Rent subsidies—United States. 2. Poor as
consumers—United States. I. Title.
HD7288.83.H36 1987 363.5'8 86-32638

ISBN 978-0-521-32752-7 hardback
ISBN 978-0-521-07446-9 paperback

Contents

List of tables *page* vii
Acknowledgments ix

1 Introduction 1
 1.1 Current subsidy programs 2
 1.2 Methodological approach 9
 1.3 The data 10
2 Evolution of the methodology 12
 2.1 The methodological approach 13
 2.2 Evolution of the methodology 13
 2.3 Summary 21
3 The model 23
 3.1 An overview of intertemporal consumer theory 23
 3.2 An intertemporal model of household
 consumption behavior 26
 3.3 Direct benefit 29
 3.4 Changes in consumption patterns 35
4 Estimation procedures 37
 4.1 Length of life 37
 4.2 Length of participation in a subsidized housing
 program 38
 4.3 The real rate of interest 39
 4.4 Relative prices 40
 4.5 Household income 44
 4.6 Rents and quantities of subsidized housing 53
 4.7 The parameters of the utility function 61
5 Empirical results 70
 5.1 Changes in consumption patterns and magnitude
 of benefits to participating households 70

	5.2	Distribution of benefits	84
	5.3	Comparisons with previous work	93
6	Summary and conclusion		96
	6.1	Summary	96
	6.2	Conclusion	106

Appendix A	109
Appendix B	116
Notes	120
Bibliography	126
Index	137

Tables

1.1	HUD-subsidized rental housing units at end of year	*page* 4
4.1	Definition of terms used in income regressions	49
4.2	Estimated relationships between natural log of 1977 total household income and household characteristics by household types	50
4.3	Definition of terms used in rent regressions	55
4.4	Estimated relationships between monthly gross rent and housing unit characteristics by race – ordinary and weighted least-squares results	57
4.5	Homoskedasticity test	60
4.6	Unconstrained estimates of the parameters of the utility function by household type	64
4.7	Constrained estimates of the parameters of the utility function by household type	66
5.1	Aggregate effects of government-subsidized housing programs	72
5.2	Aggregate effects of replacing government-subsidized rental housing programs with unrestricted cash grants	75
5.3	Aggregate future consumption effects of subsidized housing programs and alternative policies – households in any subsidy program	78
5.4	Aggregate future consumption effects of subsidized housing programs and alternative policies – households in public housing	80
5.5	Aggregate future consumption effects of subsidized housing programs and alternative policies – households in other subsidy programs	82
5.6	Comparison of characteristics of families in all subsidy programs combined, low-rent public housing,	

and other subsidized housing programs to the
population of U.S. households 85

5.7 Distribution of benefits by income class for one- to
two-person households in all subsidy programs
combined 86

5.8 Distribution of benefits by income class for three- to
four-person households in all subsidy programs
combined 86

5.9 Distribution of benefits by income class for five or
more person households in all subsidy programs
combined 87

5.10 Distributive effects of government-subsidized rental
housing programs 88

5.11 Differences in estimated real benefit between
households one standard deviation above and below
the mean value of explanatory variable 90

5.12 Additional benefit regressions 91

5.13 Test for nonlinearities 92

A.1 Prices of nonhousing goods and housing services by
SMSA and region 110

B.1 Distribution of benefits by income class for one- to
two-person households in low-rent public housing 117

B.2 Distribution of benefits by income class for three- to
four-person households in low-rent public housing 117

B.3 Distribution of benefits by income class for five or
more person households in low-rent public housing 118

B.4 Distribution of benefits by income class for one- to
two-person households in other subsidized housing
programs 118

B.5 Distribution of benefits by income class for three- to
four-person households in other subsidized housing
programs 119

B.6 Distribution of benefits by income class for five or
more person households in other subsidized housing
programs 119

Acknowledgments

This book is a revision of my University of Virginia Ph.D. dissertation. For the dissertation I was co-winner of the 1983 Irving Fisher Award. I would like to thank a number of people who helped in the preparation of both the dissertation and this book.

First and most importantly, my deepest thanks and appreciation go to Edgar O. Olsen, Professor of Economics at the University of Virginia and chairman of my dissertation committee. He has read numerous drafts of this work and from the beginning of the project was a constant source of ideas, useful criticism, and encouragement. Ed's active interest in this work has been indispensable.

Wake Epps and Jonathan Skinner were the other members of my dissertation committee. They and my colleagues at Wake Forest University, especially Van Wagstaff, John Moorhouse, Donald Frey, Tony Elavia, and John Wood, provided helpful comments and support. Linda May and other members of the Wake Forest University Computer Center provided much needed computing assistance.

Wake Forest University generously provided me with a course reduction in the fall of 1985 and financial support for the preparation of the revised manuscript. Faye Kisel of the Wake Forest economics department cheerfully provided both secretarial assistance and a friendly ear.

Finally, I want to thank my husband, J. Daniel Hammond. He read and proofread, critiqued, and edited every page of both the dissertation and the book. He has been my staunchest supporter and most steadfast colleague. My special thanks also go to Joseph, Patrick, and Jane Marie, who made the whole process a lot more challenging and a lot more fun.

<div align="right">Claire Holton Hammond</div>

Winston-Salem, North Carolina
September 1986

Introduction

Government housing subsidy programs for low- and moderate-income families have been affecting the well-being and consumption patterns of families all over the United States since the late 1930s. Nevertheless, there is little empirical evidence on the total benefits of, and consumption changes due to, this government intervention designed to further the national goal of a "decent home and a suitable living environment for every American family."[1] This is true despite the fact that a large body of microdata on government housing subsidy programs is available in the Annual Housing Survey (AHS), which has been conducted by the U.S. Bureau of the Census for the U.S. Department of Housing and Urban Development (HUD) since 1973.

The purpose of this study is to use these data for 1977 to evaluate the benefits of federal, state, and local government-subsidized rental housing programs taken as a whole. Specifically, I want to determine:

1. The direct benefits of the programs to participating families.
2. The changes in consumption patterns resulting from these programs. It is expected that nonparticipating families also benefit from the programs, especially when the programs provide improved housing to low-income families. I am not able to estimate directly these benefits to nonparticipating families. Therefore, I investigate them indirectly by estimating how much more or less housing and nonhousing goods are consumed by participating families than would be consumed in the absence of the programs.
3. The distribution of the benefits; that is, the relationship between mean household benefit and household income; household size; age, education, sex, and race of head of household; and the geographic location of the family. Furthermore, I want to determine the extent to which equally situated families receive equal or different benefits.

1

Previous studies of the benefits of government housing subsidy programs have focused on single housing programs. The defect of this approach is that it is likely to give a distorted view of the equity of the programs. Weicher (1979) points out that when individual programs are analyzed separately they have all been found to be inequitable: A program provides benefits to the relatively small number of participating households but nothing to the large number of equally eligible households who are not accepted into that particular program. It is possible, however, that some of the eligible population excluded from one program are being served by another housing program. By focusing on government housing subsidy programs as a whole instead of on individual programs, it will be possible to more adequately assess the overall distributive effects of our government housing policies.

This approach does not take into account the existence of other government subsidy programs, for example, food stamps, which may address the distributive or equity failures of government housing subsidy programs. In addition, government subsidy programs for homeowners are omitted. With the Annual Housing Survey it is impossible to determine if a homeowner family is a participant in a housing subsidy program. The result of the omission of homeowner subsidy programs is that the analysis of the overall distributive effects of government housing subsidy programs will be incomplete. For example, studies show that the special income tax provisions relating to homeownership have significant distributional impact (see Aaron 1970 and 1972). Another important homeowner subsidy is HUD's Section 235 homeownership assistance program.[2] In 1977 this program subsidized 292,814 families or 11 percent of the total number of families participating in HUD-sponsored housing subsidy programs.

The remainder of this chapter describes the major government rental housing subsidy programs, the methodological approach to be used in the analysis, and the data. Chapter 2 documents the evolution of the methodology used for estimating an appropriate measure of benefit of housing subsidy programs. In Chapter 3 the model is presented; in Chapter 4 the estimation procedures are described; and in Chapter 5 the results are discussed. Chapter 6 includes the summary and conclusions of the study.

1.1 Current subsidy programs

Numerous federal housing programs, varying in method and scope, have evolved over the past fifty years.[3] The principal federal rental housing subsidy programs currently in operation include:

1. Low-rent public housing
2. Section 236 rental housing assistance
3. Rent supplements
4. Section 8 new construction/substantial rehabilitation
5. Section 8 existing housing

Table 1.1 describes the development and current status of these programs as of 1984. All of these programs are administered by HUD. They differ according to the subsidy mechanism used and the extent of the subsidy. The primary goal of the programs is to induce low- and moderate-income families to occupy better housing than they would with equally costly unrestricted cash grants. An additional goal of all the programs except Section 8 existing housing is to encourage housing construction and construction employment. The remainder of this section will describe the particular characteristics of the federal housing subsidy programs listed above.[4]

Low-rent public housing

Low-rent public housing, established by the U.S. Housing Act of 1937, was the first major federal housing subsidy program. Originally, it provided federal funds to local public housing authorities (known as LHAs) for the construction of apartments to be provided to low-income families at reduced rents. Since 1937 the original statute creating low-rent public housing has been amended several times. In 1965 Section 23 of the amended 1937 act permitted local public housing authorities to lease privately owned units for the public housing program.[5] In 1967 the turnkey mechanism was instituted that allowed the local housing authorities to purchase privately owned and developed units for the program. In 1969 the Brooke Amendment limited the rent of a participating family to 25 percent of its annual adjusted income.[6] At the same time, additional federal payments to help pay operating costs were authorized.

In 1973 new low-rent public housing activity was suspended when a national moratorium on all housing assistance programs was called by President Nixon. After review, the public housing program was revived in 1976 in essentially the same form as before. There are two exceptions. First, all new projects must be purchased under the turnkey mechanism. Second, the Section 23 leased public housing program has been replaced by the new Section 8 program.

In 1977 there were 1,174,000 housing units in the public housing program (see Table 1.1). Of this total, 101,000 were leased public

TABLE 1.1

HUD-SUBSIDIZED RENTAL HOUSING UNITS AT END OF YEAR
(Cumulative)

Fiscal Year	Public Housing	Section 23 Leased Units in Public Housing Total	Rent Supplement	Rental Housing Assistance (Section 236)	Lower Income Housing Assistance (Section 8) New Construction/ Subs. Rehab.	Existing	Total
1941–1956	343,907					———	343,907
1957	365,896						365,896
1958	374,172						374,172
1959	401,467						401,467
1960	425,481						425,481
1961	465,481						465,481
1962	482,714						482,714
1963	511,047						511,047
1964	539,841						539,841
1965	577,347						577,347
1966	608,554	(238)[a]					608,554
1967	639,631	(5,060)	930				640,561
1968	687,336	(27,947)	2,731				690,067

TABLE 1.1 - Continued

1969	767,723	(62,089)	12,299				780,022
1970	830,454	(76,816)	30,804	5,437			866,695
1971	892,651	(92,629)	57,786	32,322			982,759
1972	989,419	(106,633)	92,070	98,699			1,180,188
1973	1,047,000	(127,000)	118,184	191,261			1,356,445
1974	1,109,000	(142,000)	147,847	293,831			1,550,678
1975	1,151,000	(143,000)	165,326	400,360			1,716,686
1976	1,167,000	(135,000)	177,645	439,872	5,427	125,044	1,914,988
1977	1,174,000	(101,000)	179,908	543,360	31,595	421,540	2,350,403
1978	1,173,000	(92,000)	171,598	544,515	85,339	581,264	2,555,716
1979	1,178,000	(70,000)	178,891	541,460	117,952	526,339	2,818,315
1980	1,192,000	(52,000)	164,992	538,285	334,321	818,990	3,048,588
1981	1,204,000	(40,000)	157,779	537,206	474,465	844,462	3,217,912
1982	1,224,000	(34,000)	153,355	536,531	571,298	955,385	3,440,569
1983	1,250,000	(33,000)	76,919	533,469	664,395	1,085,509	3,610,292
1984	1,331,908	(28,000)	55,606	530,735	730,148	1,179,664	3,828,061

SOURCE: Wayne Baker, Housing Budget Office, U.S. Department of Housing and Urban Development, Washington, D.C., October, 1985.

[a]Represents number of public housing units in Section 23 programs. Figures are excluded from totals.

housing units. By 1984 the number of public housing units had increased to 1,331,908, whereas leased units in that total had declined to 28,000.

Low-rent public housing is generally limited to low- and moderate-income families or to low-income elderly, handicapped, or displaced individuals. Income eligibility limits for families of each size are set by each local public housing authority and are approved by HUD. They are usually about 68 percent of the area median income for a family of four.

Section 236 rental housing assistance program

This program was established by the Housing and Urban Development Act of 1968 as Section 236 of an amended National Housing Act of 1934. In the Section 236 program, participating families pay rent sufficient to cover operating expenses of their units plus mortgage amortization costs at 1 percent interest rate, or 25 percent of their adjusted incomes, whichever is greater. HUD pays the difference between the tenant's rent and the market rent of the unit, which is the amount needed to cover mortgage amortization costs at the market interest rate.

To be eligible for Section 236 housing assistance, family income may be no more than 135 percent of the area income eligibility limit for low-rent public housing. Families whose rent in the program is greater than 25 percent of their adjusted income may receive additional rent subsidies either through the rent supplement program or through the "deep subsidy" provisions of the Section 236 program.

New activity in the Section 236 program was suspended in 1973 and has not been reinstated. In 1977 there were 543,360 housing units in the Section 236 program (see Table 1.1).

Rent supplement program

This program was established by Section 101 of the Housing and Urban Development Act of 1965. It is always used in conjunction with another government housing program, for example, the Section 236 rental housing assistance program or the Section 221(d)(3) program, which provides financial incentives to private developers to build multi-family housing. Under the rent supplement program, the federal government makes monthly rental payments to the landlord on behalf of the tenant.

To be eligible, family income must be less than the local income

limit for eligibility for low-rent public housing. In addition, the family must have an elderly or handicapped head or spouse, a veteran or member of the armed forces, or have been displaced by urban renewal. Participating families contribute 25 percent of their income to rent, with the government paying the difference between the tenant contribution and the full rent of the apartment.

New activity in the rent supplement program was suspended in 1973 and has not been reinstated. In 1977 there were 179,908 housing units in the rent supplement program.

Section 8 new construction/substantial rehabilitation program

This program was established by the Housing and Community Development Act of 1974 as Section 8 of an amended U.S. Housing Act of 1937. This program operates much like leased public housing. Its purpose is to ensure that lower-income families are able to afford "decent" housing and to encourage housing construction. Under the program the federal government subsidizes rents for apartments built or substantially rehabilitated by public or private developers. Contracts between the project sponsors and HUD are for five years, renewable for twenty to forty years depending on the type of sponsor and financing.

The landlords choose their tenants, who must meet certain income standards depending on family size. The maximum allowable income ranges from 50 percent of area median income for a single person to 80 percent of the area median for a family of four to 100 percent of the area median for a family of eight or more. For each project, HUD also requires that at least 30 percent of the initial tenants have "very low income," defined as income below 50 percent of area median income for a family of four. Virtually all tenant families are required to pay 25 percent of their adjusted income as rent. HUD pays the project manager the difference between the tenant contribution and the HUD-established allowable rent for the unit. In 1977 there were 31,595 units in the Section 8 new construction/substantial rehabilitation program. In 1984 this had risen to 730,148 units (see Table 1.1).

Section 8 existing housing program

Although this program was authorized by the same statute that established the Section 8 new construction/substantial rehabilitation program, the two programs are significantly different and are administered separately by HUD. The Section 8 existing housing program is

designed to rely on the initiative of lower-income families to provide themselves with better housing. Under the program the eligible family receives a rent subsidy that is applied to an apartment of its own choosing in the private market. The family is free to select the type of housing and location as long as the unit meets certain quality standards and rents for no more than the HUD-established "fair market rent." In addition, the family is allowed to stay in place if its present unit meets these restrictions.

Income eligibility is the same as for Section 8 new construction/substantial rehabilitation. The tenant rental contribution is 25 percent of income in almost all cases. The difference between the rent and the tenant contribution is paid by HUD to the local agency administering the program, which in turn pays the landlord on behalf of the tenant.

This program and its predecessor (Section 23 existing) are unique among federal housing assistance programs. The subsidy is associated with the assisted family and is not tied to a particular housing unit. Its purpose is to improve the housing of low-income families, not to encourage housing construction. The program is like a price subsidy with upper and lower limits on housing quality. The fair market rent restriction sets the upper limit and the quality standards set the lower limit. In 1977 there were 421,540 units in the program. In 1984 this had grown to 1,179,664 units.

State and local government housing subsidy programs

In addition to the federal subsidy programs, state and local governments also provide, but on a much smaller scale, rental housing assistance to low- and moderate-income families. The collection of information on each of these programs would be a tremendous undertaking. Consequently, I will limit the description to New York State's Mitchell–Lama housing program, which is probably the largest and has received a certain amount of attention in the literature (see DeSalvo 1975).

The Mitchell–Lama program was established in 1955 in order to subsidize the housing of middle-income families, especially those with children. Under the program the state provides private developers of rental housing with long-term, low-interest loans and property tax exemptions in return for reduced rents for eligible tenants. Financing of the program is provided by New York's Housing and Development Administration from state or city bond issues. Income eligibility depends on family size. For families of four or less, annual income may not exceed six times annual rent. For families with more than four persons, income may not exceed seven times annual rent.

The great majority of Mitchell–Lama projects are located in New York City. In 1968 New York City's projects provided subsidized rents for 57,000 households.

1.2 Methodological approach

This study employs a simple, general equilibrium model directly based on models developed by DeSalvo (1971a, 1975), Kraft and Olsen (1977), Murray (1975), Olsen (1972), and Olsen and Barton (1983). A Hicksian price equivalent measure of consumer surplus is used to estimate the value of the programs to participating families. This involves selecting a utility function for the participating families, estimating its parameters, and comparing the utility surface attained under participation in the programs with the utility surfaces attained under certain alternatives to participation. An intertemporal utility function is used, which allows future income and prices to affect current consumption decisions. The model also acknowledges the fact that current household consumption will be less than current income if the household is saving and greater than current income if the household is borrowing.

Previous studies that have used a Hicksian measure of consumer surplus assume a one-year planning horizon and work with a one-year utility function. In addition, they assume that all current income is spent in the current period. The benefit measure is derived by comparing utility levels given two alternative states: (1) The household participates in the housing program in the current year; and (2) the household cannot participate in the housing program in the current year. The measure of benefit derived from these alternatives is interpreted as the size of the unrestricted cash grant that, if given to the family in place of participation in the housing program, would leave the family as well off without the program as participating in it.

Within an intertemporal, or multiperiod, framework household expectations of the future, including plans to participate in a housing program, are allowed to affect current consumption patterns and utility levels. Consequently, the selection of alternative states to compare and determination of the appropriate benefit measure are more complicated.

In this research the benefit measure is derived by comparing utility levels given two alternative expectations about participation in a housing program:

1. Up to the beginning of the current year the household plans to participate in a housing program for a certain number of years

that include the current year but no future years. Under the first alternative these plans are fulfilled.

2. Up to the beginning of the current year the household plans to participate in a housing program for a certain number of years that include the current year but no future years. Under the second alternative the household learns at the beginning of the current year that the program will be immediately and permanently terminated.

The measure of benefit derived from these alternatives is interpreted as the size of the one-year cash grant, which enables the household to reach a level of utility without participation in a housing subsidy program in the current year or beyond that is identical to the utility level reached given participation in the current year but no future years. Benefit so defined measures the value a participating family places on one more year's operation of the housing subsidy program.

1.3 The data

The data are from the national sample of the 1977 Annual Housing Survey.[7] These data include extensive information about 76,000 housing units and their occupants selected randomly from the approximately 68.7 million housing units identified in the 1970 census. The survey was conducted over a four-month period centered about October 1977. Interviewers from the Census Bureau visited each household occupying a housing unit in the sample. For vacant units information was obtained from landlords, rental agents, or neighbors. In this research owner-occupied housing units and housing units that were vacant or occupied by people whose usual place of residence is elsewhere are excluded. Of the 16,759 rental households remaining, an additional 5,251 households (31 percent) are excluded for several reasons. Housing units located in hotels, rooming houses, trailers, mobile homes, commercial establishments, and medical offices are excluded. Because of the widespread presence of rent control in New York City, housing units located in the New York City Standard Metropolitan Statistical Area (SMSA) are also excluded.

Data are collected on the characteristics of the households and the housing units they occupy. Household characteristics include household size, income, and composition and the race, sex, age, education, and income of the household head and selected other household members. For this study, households with unrelated members are excluded because of the inability to separate the characteristics of the primary

family from nonrelatives who may be roomers, boarders, lodgers, resident employees, wards, and foster children. In addition, the intertemporal model for estimating benefit (developed in Chapter 3) assumes that each household has a common planning horizon equal to 54 years, beginning at age 21 and ending at age 75. Therefore, households with heads younger than 21 or older than 74 are excluded.

Structural housing unit characteristics contained in the survey include number of rooms, type of heating and cooling equipment, kitchen and plumbing facilities, type and age of structure, and quality of neighborhood services. Financial characteristics of rental housing include contract rent, utilities, parking, and garbage collection fees.

The Annual Housing Survey microdata file identifies four census regions, each SMSA of 250,000 or more at the time of the 1970 census (125 SMSAs), metropolitan or nonmetropolitan residence, and urban and rural residence for households residing outside an identified SMSA.

In addition, the data identify whether the housing unit is in a public housing project, is private subsidized housing, or private unsubsidized housing. According to the Annual Housing Survey:

A housing unit is classified as being in a "public housing project" if the structure in which the unit is located is owned by a local housing authority or other public agency, such as a housing and redevelopment authority or a housing development agency, and operated as public housing. These organizations may receive subsidies from the Federal or State government but the local agency owns the property. All other housing units are classified as "private housing." Private housing units are further classified by whether the unit is subsidized; that is, the respondent pays a lower rent because a Federal, State, or local government program pays part of the cost of construction, building mortgage, or operating expenses. (U.S. Department of Commerce 1979a, Appendix A, p. APP-19)

The figures depend on the respondent's knowledge and ability to correctly classify his housing unit as public, private subsidized, or private unsubsidized.[8] In this study households are excluded who respond "no answer" to the questions regarding the classification of their housing units according to subsidy received.

Evolution of the methodology

Studies evaluating the tenant benefits of housing subsidy programs can be classified according to the benefit measure employed in the study. The benefit to participating families has frequently been measured by the subsidy given. For rental housing programs, this subsidy is the difference between the market rent of the housing unit and the rent paid by the family. Prescott (1967), Smolensky (1968), Bish (1969), and Aaron (1972, p. 122) are examples of studies that use this measure. In general, this benefit measure is unsatisfactory because the participating family is not indifferent between all dwellings providing the same subsidy. Therefore, different dwellings providing the same subsidy should not have the same measured benefit.

A second measure that has been used for evaluating housing programs is Marshall's consumer surplus measure. See, for example, Olsen and Prescott (1969), Olsen (1972), and Mayo (1980). With this method, benefit is defined as the change in consumer's surplus, as measured along a Marshallian demand curve, which results from changes in housing prices and consumption due to participation in a housing program. A major drawback of this measure is that it has no natural interpretation except under the restrictive assumption of zero income elasticity of demand for housing.

A third measure of tenant benefit is the Hicksian price equivalent variation. With this measure, tenant benefit is defined as the amount of additional income the participating family requires in order to be as well off without the housing subsidy program as participating in it. Unlike the other two measures, this measure corresponds to a conceptually useful definition of benefit.[1]

To estimate the equivalent variation measure of benefit generally involves selecting a utility function for participating families, estimating its parameters, and comparing the utility surfaces attained under participation with the utility surfaces attained in the absence of participation.[2] Since 1975 there have been many attempts to estimate this benefit mea-

sure using different utility functions with varying degrees of generality, and using increasingly sophisticated techniques for estimating the parameters of the utility function and market rent of the subsidized housing units. The purpose of this chapter is to critically examine the evolution of the indifference map approach to measuring benefit and its empirical application to rental housing subsidy programs.

2.1 The methodological approach

Standard practice in housing studies that have used a Hicksian benefit measure has been to assume the existence of two composite commodities, generally labeled "housing services" and "all other goods and services." The participating household's preferences are assumed to be representable by a particular utility function, $U = f(H, X)$ where H is the quantity of housing services and X is quantity of all other goods and services.

By maximizing this utility function subject to the family's budget constraint, an indirect utility function can be derived, $U' = g(Y, P_h, P_x)$, which gives the highest level of utility that can be obtained given the family's income, Y, and the market prices of housing services and all other goods, P_h and P_x, respectively. Similarly, we can solve $U' = g(Y, P_h, P_x)$ for Y as a function of U', P_h, and P_x. $Y = g^{-1}(U', P_h, P_x)$ gives the level of income the family must have in order to attain utility level U', given market prices of H and X.

Participation in the housing subsidy program allows the family to achieve a certain level of utility, $U_s = f(H_s, X_s)$, where H_s is the quantity of housing services offered in the program and X_s is the quantity of all other goods and services that are purchased by the family after it has paid its subsidized rent. The family will participate in the housing program if $U_s > U'_0$, where $U'_0 = g(Y_0, P_h, P_x)$. The Hicksian measure of benefit is the difference between the amount of income that allows the family to attain U_s without the program and Y_0, the family's initial income. Thus, benefit is $B = g^{-1}(U_s, P_h, P_x) - Y_0$. In order to estimate B for every participating family, one must first specify an explicit utility function. Each utility function imposes different restrictions on behavior and differs with respect to ease of estimation and benefit calculation.

2.2 Evolution of the methodology

DeSalvo (1971a) was the first to adapt this methodology to housing subsidy programs. He assumes a Cobb–Douglas utility function, $U = H^\beta X^{1-\beta}$ where β is the rent-to-income ratio of a household that maximizes subject to the usual linear budget constraint, $P_h H + P_x X = Y$. The

drawback of the Cobb–Douglas form is that it imposes unitary income and own price elasticities; however, its parameter is easy to estimate and the benefit expression derived from it is easy to calculate.

DeSalvo shows the benefit formula to be

$$B = \left(\frac{P_h H_s}{\beta}\right)^{\beta} \left(\frac{P_x X_s}{1-\beta}\right)^{1-\beta} - Y$$

where $P_h H_s$ is the market rent of the subsidized housing unit and $P_x X_s$ is the expenditure on nonhousing goods by the participating family. Assuming the household spends all of its income Y in the current year, $P_x X_s$ can be measured as the excess of annual income over the tenant contribution to rent. To implement DeSalvo's methodology, it is necessary to have observations on market rent of the unit, tenant contribution to rent, annual household income, and the parameter β, the household's rent-to-income ratio in the absence of any subsidy.

DeSalvo (1975) applies this methodology in an analysis of New York City's Mitchell–Lama middle-income housing program. His data include values for tenant rent and income; however, rents for the units in the Mitchell–Lama program are crudely estimated by the opinions of experts within the New York State Urban Development Corporation. To estimate β, a function is estimated relating the rent-to-income ratio to household size, and age and sex of head of household from a sample consisting of households living in unsubsidized, non-rent-controlled housing. The estimated relationship is then used to predict the rent-to-income ratio β for each subsidized family.

DeSalvo finds that the mean tenant benefit of this program was $450 per year in 1968. In order to investigate the distribution of those benefits, he regresses estimated annual benefit on annual household income, household size, and age and sex of head of household. He finds a significant relationship between tenant benefit and household size, age, and sex of head of household. Larger households and those with older heads receive greater benefits. Those households with female heads receive lower benefits. The negative relationship between benefit and household income is not significant. The large standard error of estimate signifies that net benefit varies considerably among participating families similar in other respects.

DeSalvo also compares the means of characteristics of Mitchell–Lama households to those of households residing in unsubsidized, non-rent-controlled housing in New York City in 1968. On average, the participating households are found to be little different from nonparticipating households in terms of annual income, household size, age of head, and proportion of female-headed households.

Kraft and Olsen (1977) apply the DeSalvo methodology in a study of the benefits of public housing in five cities using a more sophisticated method for estimating market rent than reliance on expert opinion. Like DeSalvo they evaluate tenant benefits and their distribution, and they also investigate consumption changes resulting from participation in the public housing program. They use the demand functions corresponding to the Cobb–Douglas utility function to predict housing and nonhousing consumption of public housing tenants in the absence of this program. Their sample includes 333 households in public housing and 168 households in private housing in Boston, Pittsburgh, St. Louis, San Francisco, and Washington in 1972.

The Kraft–Olsen study, following DeSalvo, employs a Cobb–Douglas utility function. To estimate benefit and changes in consumption using this specification, the model requires values for household income, tenant rent, expenditure on housing in the absence of participation, market rent of public housing units, market prices of housing and nonhousing goods in the different cities, and the parameter of the utility function. Kraft and Olsen have data on household income and tenant rent. They estimate market prices from Bureau of Labor Statistics (BLS) cross-sectional indexes and predict the remaining variables.

The parameter of the utility function is predicted using essentially the same method as DeSalvo used. The rent-to-income ratio of households renting housing on the private market is regressed on race, sex, and age of head of household and number of household members for each city. The characteristics of public housing tenants in the different cities are substituted into these equations to predict the rent-to-income ratio for the participating households. To predict the expenditure on housing in the absence of the program, the predicted rent-to-income ratio of the participating households is multiplied by household income. Expenditure on nonhousing goods is again measured as the difference between income and housing expenditure.

To estimate market rent, Kraft and Olsen rely on previously estimated relationships between market rent and housing characteristics calculated by Gillingham (1973) for each of the five cities in 1960. The housing characteristics include age of structure, number of rooms, number of bathrooms, condition of unit, inclusion in rent of furnishings, air conditioning, and stove, presence of hot water, central heat, parking, and elevator, number of persons in unit, and race of head of household. The housing characteristics of the public housing units in the sample are substituted into Gillingham's hedonic rent equations and adjusted with BLS housing price indices to predict market rents in 1972.

Average net tenant benefit for the sample is estimated at $648 per year. It is found that public housing tenants in the sample consume on average 11 percent more housing and 18 percent more nonhousing goods than they would have in the absence of public housing.

These results are not based on a random sample of the population of public housing tenants. In order to get a better estimate of mean benefit for the public housing population, net tenant benefit and the proportional changes in housing and nonhousing consumption are regressed on household characteristics, including income, race, sex, and age of head and number of household members, using data from the sample. The mean characteristics of all public housing families are substituted into the estimated relationship on the assumption that the relationships between benefit and consumption changes and household characteristics for the sample are good estimates of the relationships for the population.

The mean tenant benefit using this procedure is $972 per year. Aggregate consumption of housing and nonhousing goods is estimated to increase 33 and 14 percent, respectively.

In order to investigate the distribution of benefits, estimated tenant benefit is regressed on household income and income squared, household size and size squared, age of head and age squared, and sex and race of the head of household. The results indicate that mean tenant benefit is negatively related to household income and positively related to household size. Female- and black-headed households receive smaller benefits. Benefit is not found to vary significantly with age but does vary widely among similarly situated households. Finally, the results suggest that there are nonlinearities in the relationship between benefit and household characteristics.

In response to President Nixon's 1973 moratorium on new activity in subsidized housing programs, the National Housing Policy Review Taskforce conducted a study designed to assess the 1972 performance of the suspended programs.[3] Evaluation includes application of the methodology developed by DeSalvo and Kraft and Olsen in order to determine the following: (1) the benefit of the programs to the participating households as measured by the amount of additional income the household would accept in lieu of participation; (2) the annual cost to the taxpayers for the participating households; and (3) the extent to which households consume more housing services than they would in the absence of the programs.

Of the programs evaluated, three are rental housing subsidy programs – low-rent public housing, the Section 236 housing assistance program, and the rent supplement program. The major conclusions of

the study regarding these programs are as follows. Average annual direct benefit to participating families is estimated at $912 for public housing, $499 for Section 236 housing, and $607 for the rent supplement program. Average annual taxpayer cost for the participating families is $1,650 for public housing, $1,051 for Section 236 housing, and $1,310 for the rent supplement program. Consumption of housing services increases 71 percent for public housing and 51 percent for Section 236 housing. Consumption of nonhousing goods shows a 16 percent increase for low-rent public housing and no change for Section 236 housing.[4]

Not holding other household characteristics constant, it is found that minority families are served to a greater degree as a percent of total eligible families than other low- and moderate-income families. Almost 70 percent of households in the public housing and rent supplement programs are female headed. A household's geographical location significantly affects its chances of participating in a subsidized housing program. Households located in the South have a greater chance of being served than households of equal income located elsewhere. Similarly, households located in the Far West, Mountain, Plains, and mid-Atlantic states have a lesser chance of participating than households located elsewhere.

Among households in low-rent public housing, it is found that average benefit tends to increase as income falls. However, there is great variation in benefit among participating families with similar incomes. For the Section 236 program, average benefit increases weakly with income. For the rent supplement program, probability of being served decreases slightly with income.

Murray (1975) extends the methodology in a study of tenant benefits from eighty-six public housing projects in seven cities in 1968. He estimates the parameters of three utility functions, the Cobb–Douglas, the constant elasticity of substitution (CES), and the generalized CES, in order to test the hypothesis that the true specification is Cobb–Douglas or ordinary CES. He also estimates benefits using two of these utility functions in order to determine "whether the Cobb–Douglas specification serves as a useful approximation to the generalized CES even when it is statistically rejected as the true specification" (p. 784).

The generalized CES utility function is of the form $U = (aH^b + X^c)^d$, where H and X are quantities of housing services and nonhousing goods, respectively; a, b, and c are parameters of the utility function; and d is an arbitrary scale factor. This form of the utility function allows both income and price elasticities to vary. It reduces to the

ordinary CES function if $b = c = 1/d$. The ordinary CES function implies unitary income elasticity but does not impose unitary own price elasticities. The Cobb–Douglas form, which imposes both unitary income and price elasticities, is a limiting case of the generalized CES form. However, unlike the Cobb–Douglas form, the generalized CES does not provide an explicit formula for benefits. An iterative computer program can be used to estimate benefits given the generalized CES specification to the desired degree of accuracy.

Murray's sample is stratified into nine family compositions depending on household size and number of minors. Separate utility functions are estimated for each composition. Data on rents and incomes of participating families within each composition prior to moving into public housing are used to estimate the parameters of the utility functions.

The data are from public housing applications that report income, rent prior to participation, subsidized rent, and household characteristics. In addition to this information and the parameter estimates, benefit estimation requires values for prices of housing and nonhousing goods and the market rent of the public housing unit. Price indices are again based on BLS prices. Market rents are estimated by adapting an hedonic regression equation relating market rent to housing characteristics estimated by Olsen (1972) for New York City in 1968. Cross-sectional price indices were used to adjust the regression equation to other cities.

From tests for the correct specification of the utility function, Murray (1975) concludes:

We cannot frequently reject the hypothesis that the true specification is [ordinary] CES, but we uniformly reject the Cobb–Douglas specification. One interpretation of these results is that we cannot reject the hypothesis of unitary income elasticity but can reject the hypothesis of unitary price elasticity. (p. 782)

Furthermore, Murray finds that the benefit estimates based on the Cobb–Douglas and generalized CES specifications exhibit significantly different distributional patterns, although there is not much difference in average benefit. For the generalized CES specification, average constant-dollar benefit varies from a low of $720 per year for single persons to a high of $1,500 per year for six-person households with five minors. For the Cobb–Douglas specification, average benefit ranges from $624 for single persons to $1,428 for five-person households with four minors.

To determine the distribution of benefits, constant-dollar benefit is regressed against real income, age, and race of head, family composition, and city of residence for both the Cobb–Douglas and generalized CES benefit estimates. The results differ according to the specification. Income coefficients are negative and significant with generalized CES, but positive or insignificant with the Cobb–Douglas specification. For

both specifications nonwhites receive greater benefits; benefit rises with family size and varies widely across cities. Murray (1975) concludes that the Cobb–Douglas specification is not an adequate substitution for or approximation to the generalized CES.[5]

In an attempt to use a more general utility function than either the Cobb–Douglas or the ordinary CES, but one that yields a more easily estimated benefit formula than the generalized CES, Olsen and Barton (1983) assume a Stone–Geary (sometimes called a displaced Cobb–Douglas) function in their study of public housing in New York City. The Stone–Geary utility function is of the form $U = (H - \beta_h)^\gamma (X - \beta_x)^{1-\gamma}$, where H and X are quantities of housing and nonhousing goods, respectively, the parameter γ is the marginal propensity to spend on housing, and β_h and β_x are displacement parameters. The Stone–Geary utility function is more general than the Cobb–Douglas because it permits price and income elasticities to vary with prices and income, although they monotonically approach unity as income increases. Furthermore, the Stone–Geary function, unlike the generalized CES function, leads to an explicit benefit formula.

Olsen and Barton show that the benefit formula for the Stone–Geary utility function is

$$B = [(P_h H_s - P_h \beta_h / \gamma]^\gamma [(P_x X_s - P_x \beta_x / (1 - \gamma)]^{(1-\gamma)} + P_h \beta_h + P_x \beta_x - Y$$

Thus, in order to estimate tenant benefit and changes in consumption resulting from the program, the model requires, as before, knowledge of household income, tenant rent of the public housing unit, expenditure on housing in the absence of public housing, market rent of the public housing unit, and the three parameters of the utility function.

The data from the 1965 and 1968 New York City Housing and Vacancy Surveys include information on the present rent and income and other household characteristics of public housing residents and of occupants of rent-controlled and uncontrolled private housing. To determine market rents of public housing units, annual gross rent per room of uncontrolled private rental housing is regressed on housing characteristics, including age of dwelling, condition of unit, location, number of stories, and presence of elevator, type of heat, and number of bedrooms. The estimated equations are used to predict market rent for each public housing unit in 1965 and 1968.

The parameters of the utility function are estimated for twenty household types distinguished by age, race, and marital status of head and number of household members based on a random sample of families living in uncontrolled, private rental housing.

The estimated mean annual tenant benefit to public housing families is $1,018 in 1965 and $1,160 in 1968. Aggregate consumption of hous-

ing services and nonhousing goods increases by 58 and 17 percent, respectively, in 1965 and 66 and 17 percent in 1968. The percent reduction in the market price of housing services to public housing families, measured by the proportional difference between market rent and subsidized rent, is 61 percent in 1965 and 64 percent in 1968.

This study presents the most detailed investigation of the distribution of benefits among all eligible families. Olsen and Barton (1983) regress benefit on household characteristics of public housing families and on the characteristics of all eligible families by assigning a zero benefit to an eligible family that is not served.

Among public housing families, they find a positive relationship between family size and benefit. Mean benefit is found to be greater for poorer families although the significance of income is less than in previous studies. Mean benefit does not vary significantly with race, sex, or age of head of household. There is great variation in benefit among similar families in public housing.

Among all eligible families, they find that mean benefit is significantly greater for poorer, larger, and black-headed households. In addition, benefit varies widely among similar eligible families.

The Olsen–Barton (1983) study also investigates the presence of "leap-frogging," defined as "the extent to which public housing provides its occupants with such a large benefit that their effective incomes are greater than the relevant upper income limit for eligibility. This upper income limit is approximately the income of the poorest ineligible family of the same size" (p. 327). The results indicate that in 1965 over 10 percent of public housing families had effective incomes greater than the relevant upper income limit. In 1968 almost 22 percent had effective incomes greater than the upper income limit, and 10 percent of these had effective incomes more than 20 percent greater than the upper limit for eligibility.

Olsen and Barton's study, which has been available in working paper form since 1976 [see Barton and Olsen (1976) and Olsen and Barton (1982) for early drafts], has stimulated a considerable amount of theoretical and empirical research. In fact, much of the work being done in housing benefit estimation is a direct outgrowth of the Olsen–Barton paper. For example, Olsen and Barton (1983, pp. 314–16) address the problems of selection and aggregation bias that may result from applying to subsidized families the utility function parameters estimated with data on families in unsubsidized housing. Olsen and Bierman (1982) show that selection bias is not an important objection to using this parameter estimation technique because the bias in mean benefit estimates is less than 5 percent. Aggregation bias appears to be

a more serious problem. Olsen and Agrawal (1982) find that because of aggregation bias this method of parameter estimation may overestimate benefit by 10 to 30 percent.

Reeder (1985) applies the Olsen and Barton methodology in a straightforward, comprehensive manner in his study of the benefits of the Section 8 existing housing program. His study is free of the problems of selection and aggregation bias because his data for 1,233 participating families in 1976 include values for the preprogram income and market rents paid by participating families. This allows him to estimate individualized taste parameters for program participants. Price indices are constructed from BLS and AHS data.

Reeder finds that mean tenant benefit of the Section 8 existing program is $996 in 1976. Aggregate consumption of housing services and nonhousing goods by participating families is estimated to increase by 16.3 and 50.2 percent, respectively, as a result of participation.

In order to investigate the distribution of benefits, real benefit (nominal benefit adjusted for differences in cost of living across the nation) is regressed on household real income, household size, age, sex, and ethnic group of the household head and the cost of living and metropolitan or nonmetropolitan status of the area in which the household resides. Nonlinearities are accounted for by including squared values for real income, household size, and age of the head. The results indicate that for the Section 8 existing program, real benefits are largest for the poorest and largest families and decline with increases in real income. Female-headed households receive higher real benefits while black households receive lower real benefits than similarly situated male- or white-headed households. Real benefits are also found to decline as age of the head increases beyond thirty-two. Location in a metropolitan or nonmetropolitan area is found to be an insignificant determinant of real benefit, yet households residing in higher cost areas are found to receive greater real benefit, on average. Again, a low coefficient of determination and high standard error suggest that horizontal inequities among participating families are substantial.

2.3 Summary

The standard methodology for estimating tenant benefit using the indifference map approach has evolved from the simplest one developed by DeSalvo to the more complex and rigorous methodology developed by Olsen and Barton. In each of these studies, households are assumed to spend their entire income during the current period and to maximize a utility function that depends only on the commodities consumed

during that period. Olsen and Barton criticize the restrictiveness of these assumptions. The assumptions do not allow for borrowing or lending, and they require households to be myopic since future expectations are allowed to play no role in current consumption decisions. Olsen and Barton (1983, pp. 312–13) argue that an intertemporal utility function and wealth constraint are necessary to correctly estimate benefits. This present study is an attempt to extend the methodology by following Olsen and Barton's suggestion and using an intertemporal Stone–Geary utility function. It is also an attempt to add to our knowledge of the distribution of tenant benefits by investigating rental housing subsidy programs taken as a whole.

Although previous studies investigate different programs and differ in their methods and data, a few common threads emerge with regard to rental housing subsidy programs. Each of the studies finds that, for the particular program under review, tenant benefit varies widely among participating families and among all eligible families similar in other respects. In addition, mean tenant benefit is always found to rise with household size. Tenant benefit is usually found to be negatively related to household income, although sometimes this relationship is insignificant. No common relationship emerges between mean tenant benefit and age, sex, or race of head of household.

For public housing, the most widely studied program, mean annual benefit in constant 1977 dollars varies from a low of $356 [Murray (1975) for single-person households] to highs of $671 (Kraft and Olsen 1977) and $855 (Murray for six-person households). Estimates of the aggregate increase in the consumption of housing services as a result of participation in public housing range from 33 percent (Kraft and Olsen) to 71 percent (HUD). Estimates of the aggregate increase in the consumption of nonhousing goods are more similar, varying from 14 percent (Kraft and Olsen) to 17 percent (Olsen and Barton 1983). Since these estimates refer to different times and places, uniformity is not to be expected.

The model

In this chapter, an intertemporal, general equilibrium model is developed. I assume the existence of a household intertemporal utility function of a particular form and use the corresponding derived expenditure functions to estimate the unknown parameters of the utility function. I compare the household's consumption pattern with participation in a housing program to the pattern given termination of the housing program, and estimate the size of the unrestricted cash grant that is utility equivalent to participation.

The model is based on the theory of intertemporal consumer demand originally developed by Fisher (1954) and Hicks (1946) and extended in Henderson and Quandt (1971), Malinvaud (1972), and Phlips (1974). Section 3.1 presents an overview of the intertemporal consumer theory underlying the model. The model is described in Section 3.2; in Section 3.3 the benefit measure is derived; and in Section 3.4 the method for estimating changes in consumption patterns is described.

3.1 An overview of
intertemporal consumer theory

In traditional single-period consumer demand analysis, a representative consumer is assumed to spend his entire income during the current period and to maximize a utility function that depends only on the commodities consumed during that period. This approach considers consumers to be "myopic." It assumes that the consumer ignores the fact that he is going to continue to purchase and consume in future periods. It is important to realize that a consumer's current decisions are not based solely on his perception of present realities but are also determined by expectations of the future. As Irving Fisher writes:

Valuation is a human process in which foresight enters. Coming events cast their shadows before. . . . The present worth of an article is what buyers are willing

to give for it and sellers are ready to take for it. In order that each man may logically decide what he is willing to give or take, he must have . . . some idea of the value of future benefits which that article will yield. (1954, pp. 14–5)

The introduction of time into the analysis of consumption allows us to drop the assumption of myopia and analyze the behavior of a consumer who looks into the future.

Following Hicks (1946), time is divided into discrete periods of equal length, where the periods are short enough so that variation in prices can be neglected.[1] It is assumed that a multiperiod utility function can be defined that orders the consumer's preferences among different streams of commodity bundles, where commodities are now distinguished both by nature and by date. In the general case, a consumer's utility depends upon his planned consumption of each of n goods over a planning horizon of T periods:

$$U_1 = U(q_{11}, \ldots, q_{n1}, q_{12}, \ldots, q_{n2}, \ldots, q_{1T}, \ldots, q_{nT})$$

where q_{jt} is the quantity of good j that the consumer consumes during the tth period. Usually, the planning horizon is assumed equal to the remainder of the consumer's lifetime. Theoretically, it may be any length since it is defined as the period of time for which the consumer plans in the current period.[2]

The consumer wants to choose an optimal consumption plan or program for the current period and for all subsequent periods in his planning horizon given his budget constraint. The traditional budget constraint (current income equals current expenditures) is inappropriate in an intertemporal framework due to the way decisions to save or dissave and the interest rate interact with consumption decisions. Instead, it is more appropriate to define a household's wealth constraint. The consumer expects to receive a certain stream of income over his planning horizon:

$$Y = (Y_1, Y_2, \ldots, Y_T)$$

By borrowing or lending, the consumer can transform this stream of income according to his degree of "impatience," which is defined by Fisher as "the marginal preference for present over future goods."[3]

Borrowing and lending are introduced with a number of simplifying assumptions (Henderson and Quandt 1971, p. 294). It is assumed there is only one credit instrument, a one-period bond, which is expected to yield a constant (over time) rate of return equal to r. The market for this bond is perfectly competitive. Thus, the market rate of interest r is the same for all borrowers and lenders and cannot be affected by the

activities of any one individual. Furthermore, it is assumed that there is no risk of default. Borrowers who wish to borrow for longer than one period can sell new bonds in successive periods. Lenders can reinvest their principal and interest income by buying new bonds in successive periods.

The assumption of perfect capital markets implies that households with high degrees of impatience can consume more than their current income in the present period by borrowing at the market rate of interest out of future earnings. Households with lesser degrees of impatience can trade some current consumption for future consumption by lending at the market rate of interest.[4] Thus, individual consumption plans are determined by the present value of future income over the planning horizon and are independent of how income fluctuates over the planning horizon.[5]

Assume the individual has no initial bond holdings at the beginning of his planning horizon and that he plans to have neither assets nor debts at the end of his planning horizon.[6] Assume that the consumer owns no stocks of durable goods. Instead, he purchases the desired flow of services from durable goods in each period.[7] Then, the consumer's wealth constraint is to equate the present values of his income and consumption expenditure streams over his planning horizon:

$$\sum_{t=1}^{T} \frac{Y_t}{(1+r)^{t-1}} = \sum_{t=1}^{T} \sum_{j=1}^{n} \frac{(p_{jt})(q_{jt})}{(1+r)^{t-1}}$$

where p_{jt} is the spot price of good j in period t.[8] This wealth constraint, along with the assumptions concerning the capital market, implies that a consumer may borrow any amount at any time as long as he repays his debts with interest at the end of his planning horizon. Saving or dissaving may occur in any one year, but over the entire planning horizon there is no net saving.

The consumer is assumed to regard the future with certainty and chooses in the current period an optimal consumption program by maximizing his intertemporal utility function subject to his wealth constraint. His choice depends on his expectations, or predictions, of future prices, income, and interest rates, in addition to current income and prices. Hicks (1946) analyzes the forces that shape price expectations. These include "noneconomic forces," for example, political news; information bearing on future movements of demand and supply, for example, crop reports; and actual experiences of past and present prices. Inflationary (or deflationary) expectations as well as expectations concerning changes in relative prices are taken into account by the consumer as he formulates his consumption program.

In sum, the intertemporal theory of consumer behavior assumes that an individual's current consumption expenditures and savings are a function of both present and future prices, income, and interest rates (which he regards as certain). Furthermore, a consumer not only makes his current consumption decisions in the current period, but also plans his future consumption expenditures in the current period. This does not necessarily mean that these future consumption plans will in fact be carried out. Instead, it is assumed that the individual reconsiders his current and future consumption program every period. If his expectations regarding prices, income, and interest rates are unchanged, and his tastes are unchanged, then his predetermined consumption program will be carried out. If his expectations are not verified, then the consumer will work out a new consumption program for his planning horizon based on this new information. Phlips points out that "observed behavior is therefore seen, not as following one single optimal path over time, but as a sequence of points or segments on successive optimal paths" (1974, p. 246).

3.2 An intertemporal model
of household consumption behavior

In this section an intertemporal model of household consumption behavior used to derive a measure of benefit to participating households of government subsidized housing programs is described. Assume that

1. Each household views the future as certain.
2. Each household has a planning horizon equal to the remainder of the lifetime of the head of household after his or her entry into the workforce. This planning horizon can be broken into discrete periods of one year's length.[9]
3. All market transactions take place at the beginning of each period.
4. There are two composite goods, housing services and non-housing goods, where housing services and nonhousing goods consumed in any given year are considered to be different commodities from housing services and nonhousing goods consumed in any other year.
5. The uncontrolled markets for these commodities are perfectly competitive and always in long-run equilibrium.
6. The long-run supplies of housing and nonhousing goods in all markets in all years are perfectly elastic.[10]
7. Each household's consumption is independent of any other household's consumption in any year.

8. Each household behaves as if its tastes or preferences for housing and nonhousing goods will remain unchanged.

This last assumption implies that the parameters of the utility function remain constant over time.

Consider the case of a household whose head enters the workforce during the current year and is, therefore, at the beginning of its planning horizon. In addition, suppose that the household has no intention of participating in a government-subsidized housing program at any time.[11]

Assume that the ith nonparticipating household's preferences can be represented by a Stone–Geary utility function:

$$U_{i1} = \prod_{t=1}^{L_i} (H_{it} - B_{hi})^{\gamma_i/L_i}(X_{it} - B_{xi})^{(1-\gamma_i)/L_i} \qquad (3.1)$$

where H_{it} = quantity of housing services consumed by household i in period t

X_{it} = quantity of nonhousing goods consumed by household i in period t

L_i = number of years in the planning horizon of household i, assumed equal to the number of years remaining in the life of the household head after his or her entry into the workforce

B_{hi}, B_{xi}, and γ_i are the parameters of the utility function. Assume $H_{it} > B_{hi}$; $X_{it} > B_{xi}$; and, $0 < \gamma_i < 1$. Then, the utility function is strictly quasiconcave and twice differentiable with positive first derivatives.

Assume that there is a riskless one-period bond that yields a constant real rate of return r over time. The market for this bond is perfectly competitive. Assume that the household has definite expectations about its future stream of real income, and it plans to hold neither assets nor debts at the end of its planning horizon, that is, to leave nothing for bequests. Furthermore, assume that relative prices are constant over time.[12]

Given these assumptions, the wealth constraint faced by the ith household is

$$\sum_{t=1}^{L_i} \frac{(P_{hi}H_{it}) + (P_{xi}X_{it})}{(1+r)^{t-1}} = \sum_{t=1}^{L_i} \frac{Y_{it}}{(1+r)^{t-1}} \qquad (3.2)$$

where Y_{it} is the income of household i in period t deflated to account for any inflationary expectations over time and r is the real rate of interest, assumed constant over time. P_{hi} and P_{xi} are the market prices of housing services and nonhousing goods, respectively, faced by house-

hold i in every period t, adjusted for any inflationary (or deflationary) expectations over time.

This budget constraint sets discounted expenditures on all goods over the household's planning horizon equal to discounted income over the household's planning horizon. It implies that borrowing out of future income can take place as long as all debts are paid with interest by year L_i.

The expenditures on housing services and nonhousing goods that the ith nonparticipating household plans to make in current or future years can be obtained by maximizing the household's utility function (3.1) subject to the constraint of equation (3.2). The following system of expenditure equations results[13]:

$$P_{hi}H_{it} = P_{hi}B_{hi} + \frac{\gamma_i}{L_i}(1+r)^{t-1}\left\{\sum_{t=1}^{L_i}\frac{Y_{it} - P_{hi}B_{hi} - P_{xi}B_{xi}}{(1+r)^{t-1}}\right\} \qquad (3.3)$$

for every t.

$$P_{xi}X_{it} = P_{xi}B_{xi} + \frac{1-\gamma_i}{L_i}(1+r)^{t-1}\left\{\sum_{t=1}^{L_i}\frac{Y_{it} - P_{hi}B_{hi} - P_{xi}B_{xi}}{(1+r)^{t-1}}\right\} \qquad (3.4)$$

for every t. By introducing future time periods and the ability of the consumer to borrow and lend, the model allows future prices and income to affect not only planned future expenditures but current consumption decisions as well.

The Stone–Geary utility function is selected because it is easy to estimate and to use to estimate the effects of government programs.[14] The class of utility functions to which it belongs is the only one that leads to a system of expenditure equations linear in prices and income. This linear expenditure system has had extensive practical application and, most importantly, leads to an explicit formula for the Hicksian measure of consumer surplus.[15] Furthermore, it permits price and income elasticities to vary with prices and income although the elasticities monotonically approach unity with changes in prices and income (Mayo 1981, pp. 105–6).

Other specifications used in housing studies either are not as general or do not lead to an explicit benefit formula. The Cobb–Douglas utility function imposes assumptions of unitary price and income elasticities.[16] The constant elasticity of substitution function assumes variable price elasticities but unitary income elasticity. The generalized constant elasticity of substitution utility function permits price and income elasticities to vary but does not yield an explicit benefit formula.[17] Mayo (1981) reviews housing demand analyses where alternative specifications are tried. He concludes that the demand equations

derived from the linear expenditure system perform at least as well as loglinear demand equations.[18]

The single-period Stone–Geary expenditure functions are often interpreted in the following way (see, for example, Samuelson 1947–48 and Deaton 1974). In any given year, the household first purchases necessary or subsistence quantities of each good. After these subsistence quantities have been purchased, the household allocates to each good a fixed proportion of the difference between its current income and its current subsistence expenditures.

In the multiperiod framework this interpretation must be modified. The parameters B_h and B_x can be described as the subsistence quantities of housing services and nonhousing goods consumed in every year of a household's planning horizon. I assume that these subsistence levels do not change over time. The parameter γ represents the proportion of discounted discretionary income that will be spent on housing after the subsistence quantities have been purchased. Discounted discretionary income can be defined as the amount of discounted lifetime income that remains after the household has budgeted for the subsistence levels of housing services and nonhousing goods for its entire expected lifetime. The model implies that a household will allocate an equal proportion of its discounted discretionary income to each year of its life.

3.3 Direct benefit

In this section we turn our attention to the consumption patterns of households that have chosen to participate in subsidized housing programs. The main purpose is to develop a measure of the benefit households receive from participation in the housing programs. The Hicksian price equivalent variation is used as the measure of this benefit.

In single-period models this measure is usually derived by comparing household consumption patterns and utility levels given two policy alternatives: (1) the household is allowed to participate in the housing program in the current year s; and (2) the housing authority terminates the housing program so that the household cannot participate in the current year s. The measure of benefit derived from these alternatives is the unrestricted cash grant required by the household to make nonparticipation in the current year s utility equivalent to participation in year s. In other words, the benefit measure is the value the household places on participation in the housing program for that one year s.

With an intertemporal model, household expectations of the future, including future eligibility for a housing program, are allowed to affect

current consumption patterns and utility levels. In developing an intertemporal benefit measure, the policy alternatives that are compared must be described in terms of eligibility in future years as well as in the current year.

In this study, I assume that prior to the beginning of the current year everyone believes that the program will continue for that year but not beyond. The intertemporal benefit measure is derived by comparing consumption patterns and utility levels under the following policy alternatives: (1) The housing authorities will terminate the housing programs next year, in the beginning of year $s + 1$; (2) the housing programs will terminate one year early, at the beginning of the current year s.[19] The measure of benefit derived from these alternatives is the unrestricted cash grant that allows a participating family to be as well off without participation in year s or in future years as with participation in year s, but in no future years.

Clearly, different policy alternatives could be chosen. For example, consumption patterns under the following two policy alternatives could be compared: (1) The housing programs will be continued indefinitely and the household plans to stay in its current subsidized housing unit for a given number of years, say, until death of the head of household; and (2) the housing programs will terminate immediately, in the beginning of the current year s. The benefit measure derived from these alternatives is the cash grant required in year s to make the participating family as well off with immediate termination of its program as with planned participation for the remainder of its life.

There are certain advantages in using the policy alternatives I have chosen to derive the benefit measure. This is the first foray into measuring benefits within an intertemporal framework and these alternatives have the advantage of being simple and manageable for such an undertaking. Furthermore, the benefit measure derived from these alternatives contains significant information for policymakers who must make marginal decisions because it measures the value participating families place on one more year's operation of the housing programs. Finally, this benefit measure is comparable to the benefit measure derived in the single-period models.

We begin the development of the benefit measure by determining utility levels and consumption patterns under the two policy alternatives. The utility function for a participating family in the current year s of its life cycle, given that its housing program will terminate in year $s + 1$, can be written (dropping i's for convenience):

$$U_s = (\bar{H}'_s - B_h)^{\gamma/L} \prod_{t=s+1}^{L} (H'_t - B_h)^{\gamma/L} \prod_{t=s}^{L} (X'_t - B_x)^{(1-\gamma)/L} \quad (3.5)$$

where H'_t and X'_t are the quantities of housing services and nonhousing goods consumed in year t given that the household plans to participate in a housing program in year s. \bar{H}'_s is the quantity of subsidized housing services consumed in year s.

The household maximizes this utility function subject to its wealth constraint:

$$(P'_h \bar{H}'_s) + \sum_{t=s+1}^{L} \frac{(P_h H'_t)}{(1+r)^{t-s}} + \sum_{t=s}^{L} \frac{(P_x X'_t)}{(t+r)^{t-s}}$$

$$= \sum_{t=s}^{L} \frac{Y_t}{(1+r)^{t-s}} + W_{s-1} \tag{3.6}$$

P'_h is the subsidized price paid by the participating household for a unit of housing services. It is assumed that $P'_h \leq P_h$, the market price of a unit of housing services. W_{s-1} is the value of the household's accumulated wealth at the end of year $s - 1$.

Note that in order to determine U_s and the consumption patterns chosen for year s and beyond, we need knowledge of household accumulated net assets at the end of year $s - 1$, W_{s-1}. This information is unavailable in the data used for this study. Accumulated net assets, however, depend upon previous consumption and saving decisions as well as on past income receipts and can be written

$$W_{s-1} = \sum_{t=1}^{s-1} [Y_t - (P_h H'_t + P_x X'_t)] (1+r)^{s-t} \tag{3.7}$$

Thus one way of estimating accumulated net assets in year s is by referring to the consumption program chosen in year one for years 1 through $s - 1$. In practice this method implies that we derive the benefit measure by comparing utility levels in year one instead of year s. In so doing, the need for a direct measure of W_{s-1} is eliminated.

Assume that in year 1 each participating household plans to participate in a housing program in years k through s. Different households are allowed to participate for different lengths of time. Thus, k can be different for different households. However, it is assumed that each participating household plans to maintain uninterrupted participation during years k through s. Also, assume that the household has formed definite expectations of the prices of subsidized housing services and the quantities of subsidized housing services it will receive at those prices.[20]

The participating household maximizes its utility taking into account that once it has chosen to participate in years k through s, the quantity of housing services consumed in those years is fixed. The utility function relevant in year 1 for a participating household is

$$U_1' = \prod_{t=1}^{k-1} (H_t' - B_h)^{\gamma/L} \prod_{t=k}^{s} (\bar{H}_t' - B_h)^{\gamma/L}$$

$$\times \prod_{t=s+1}^{L} (H_t' - B_h)^{\gamma/L} \prod_{t=1}^{L} (X_t' - B_x)^{(1-\gamma)/L} \qquad (3.8)$$

and the wealth constraint

$$\sum_{t=1}^{k-1} \frac{P_h H_t'}{(1+r)^{t-1}} + \sum_{t=k}^{s} \frac{P_h' \bar{H}_t'}{(1+r)^{t-1}} + \sum_{t=s+1}^{L} \frac{P_h H_t'}{(1+r)^{t-1}}$$

$$+ \sum_{t=1}^{L} \frac{P_x X_t'}{(1+r)^{t-1}} = \sum_{t=1}^{L} \frac{Y_t}{(1+r)^{t-1}} \qquad (3.9)$$

where H_t' and X_t' are the quantities of housing services and nonhousing goods consumed in year t, given that the household plans to participate in a housing program in years k through s. \bar{H}_t' is the quantity of subsidized housing services consumed in year t.

Maximizing utility function (3.8) subject to the wealth constraint (3.9), we find that the quantities of housing services and nonhousing goods that the household plans to consume over its life given participation in a housing program in years k through s can be represented by the following equations:

$$H_t' = B_h + \frac{\gamma}{(L + k\gamma - s\gamma - \gamma)} \frac{(1+r)^{t-1}}{P_h}$$

$$\times \left[\sum_{t=1}^{L} \frac{Y_t}{(1+r)^{t-1}} - \sum_{t=1}^{k-1} \frac{P_h B_h}{(1+r)^{t-1}} - \sum_{t=k}^{s} \frac{P_h' \bar{H}_t'}{(1+r)^{t-1}} \right.$$

$$\left. - \sum_{t=s+1}^{L} \frac{P_h B_h}{(1+r)^{t-1}} - \sum_{t=1}^{L} \frac{P_x B_x}{(1+r)^{t-1}} \right] \qquad (3.10)$$

for every $t \neq k, \ldots, s$

$$X_t' = B_x + \frac{1-\gamma}{(L + k\gamma - s\gamma - \gamma)} \frac{(1+r)^{t-1}}{P_x}$$

$$\times \left[\sum_{t=1}^{L} \frac{Y_t}{(1+r)^{t-1}} - \sum_{t=1}^{k-1} \frac{P_h B_h}{(1+r)^{t-1}} - \sum_{t=k}^{s} \frac{P_h' \bar{H}_t'}{(1+r)^{t-1}} \right.$$

$$\left. - \sum_{t=s+1}^{L} \frac{P_h B_h}{(1+r)^{t-1}} - \sum_{t=1}^{L} \frac{P_x B_x}{(1+r)^{t-1}} \right] \qquad (3.11)$$

for every t

Estimates of H'_t, X'_t, and \bar{H}'_t for every t can be substituted into the household's utility function (3.8) to obtain an estimate of U'_1, the level of utility given participation in a housing program in years k through s.

The next step in developing a benefit measure is to investigate household consumption plans given early termination of the housing program at the beginning of year s. Assume that the household learns of the early termination in the beginning of year s when it is reevaluating its planned consumption program for years s, $s + 1$, \ldots, L. I ask how this early termination will affect utility, and the household's consumption program for years s through L.

Note that the consumption and savings decisions made by the household in years 1, \ldots, $s - 1$ must be considered fixed. The household cannot go back in time and change its previous decisions in light of the news that the housing program will terminate one year early. The household, however, is free to change its planned consumption decisions for years s, $s + 1$, \ldots, L.

The utility function for a participating household under these conditions now becomes

$$U''_1 = \prod_{t=1}^{k-1} (H'_t - B_h)^{\gamma/L} \prod_{t=k}^{s-1} (\bar{H}'_t - B_h)^{\gamma/L} \prod_{t=s}^{L} (H''_t - B_h)^{\gamma/L}$$

$$\times \prod_{t=1}^{s-1} (X'_t - B_x)^{(1-\gamma)/L} \prod_{t=s}^{L} (X''_t - B_x)^{(1-\gamma)/L} \tag{3.12}$$

and the wealth constraint

$$\sum_{t=1}^{L} \frac{Y_t}{(1+r)^{t-1}} = \sum_{t=1}^{k-1} \frac{P_h H'_t}{(1+r)^{t-1}} + \sum_{t=k}^{s-1} \frac{P'_h \bar{H}'_t}{(1+r)^{t-1}} + \sum_{t=s}^{L} \frac{P_h H''_t}{(1+r)^{t-1}}$$

$$+ \sum_{t=1}^{s-1} \frac{P_x X'_t}{(1+r)^{t-1}} + \sum_{t=s}^{L} \frac{P_x X''_t}{(1+r)^{t-1}} \tag{3.13}$$

where H'_t, X'_t, and \bar{H}'_t are defined as previously and are considered fixed, and H''_t and X''_t are the quantities of housing services and nonhousing goods consumed in year t given that the housing program is terminated one year early at the beginning of year s.

The demand equations under this alternative are

$$H''_t = B_h + \frac{\gamma}{(L-s+1)} \frac{(1+r)^{t-1}}{P_h} \left[\sum_{t=1}^{L} \frac{Y_t}{(1+r)^{t-1}} - Q \right] \tag{3.14}$$

for every $t = s$, \ldots, L

$$X_t'' = B_x + \frac{1-\gamma}{(L-s+1)} \frac{(1+r)^{t-1}}{P_x} \left[\sum_{t=1}^{L} \frac{Y_t}{(1+r)^{t-1}} - Q \right] \quad (3.15)$$

for every $t = s, \ldots, L$

where

$$Q = \sum_{t=1}^{k-1} \frac{P_h H_t'}{(1+r)^{t-1}} + \sum_{t=k}^{s-1} \frac{P_h' \bar{H}_t'}{(1+r)^{t-1}} + \sum_{t=s}^{L} \frac{P_h B_h}{(1+r)^{t-1}}$$

$$+ \sum_{t=1}^{s-1} \frac{P_x X_t'}{(1+r)^{t-1}} + \sum_{t=s}^{L} \frac{P_x B_x}{(1+r)^{t-1}}$$

Note that Q can be described as the household's committed lifetime expenditures given participation in a housing program in years k through $s - 1$.

We are now in a position to calculate the benefit measure. The Hicksian price equivalent measure is the cash grant that, if given to the household in year s in place of participation in year s, allows the household to achieve its initial utility level, U_1'.

Let PVY″ represent the present value of the stream of expected income for year $t = 1, \ldots, L$:

$$\text{PVY}'' = \frac{Y_1}{(1+r)^0} + \frac{Y_2}{(1+r)^1} + \ldots + \frac{Y_s}{(1+r)^{s-1}}$$

$$+ \ldots + \frac{Y_L}{(1+r)^{L-1}} = \sum_{t=1}^{L} \frac{Y_t}{(1+r)^{t-1}} \quad (3.16)$$

Let PVY′ represent the present value of the stream of income plus the cash grant that enables the household to attain U_1' in spite of early termination of the housing program:

$$\text{PVY}' = \frac{Y_1}{(1+r)^0} + \frac{Y_2}{(1+r)^1} + \ldots + \frac{(Y_s + \text{CG})}{(1+r)^{s-1}}$$

$$+ \ldots + \frac{Y_L}{(1+r)^{L-1}} \quad (3.17)$$

where CG is the cash grant that exactly compensates the household for the early termination of the housing program. The measure of benefit, then, is

$$\text{CG} = (1+r)^{s-1} \ [\text{PVY}' - \text{PVY}''] \quad (3.18)$$

An estimate of PVY′ is determined in the following way. Substitut-

ing equations (3.14) and (3.15) into the utility function (3.12) allows one to form the indirect utility function:

$$
U_1 = \prod_{t=1}^{k-1} (H'_t - B_h)^{\gamma/L} \prod_{t=k}^{s-1} (\bar{H}'_t - B_h)^{\gamma/L} \prod_{t=1}^{s-1} (X'_t - B_x)^{(1-\gamma)/L}
$$

$$
\times \prod_{t=s}^{L} \left[\frac{\gamma}{L-s+1} \frac{(1+r)^{t-1}}{P_h} \left(\sum_{t=1}^{L} \frac{Y_t}{(1+r)^{t-1}} - Q \right) \right]^{\gamma/L}
$$

$$
\times \prod_{t=s}^{L} \left[\frac{1-\gamma}{L-s+1} \frac{(1+r)^{t-1}}{P_x} \left(\sum_{t=1}^{L} \frac{Y_t}{(1+r)^{t-1}} - Q \right) \right]^{(1-\gamma)/L} \tag{3.19}
$$

where U_1 is the level of utility given early termination. Solving for

$$
\text{PVY}'' = \sum_{t=1}^{L} \frac{Y_t}{(1+r)^{t-1}}
$$

from equation (3.19):

$$
\text{PVY}'' = \sum_{t=1}^{L} \frac{Y_t}{(1+r)^{t-1}} = (U_1)^{L/(L-s+1)} Z + Q \tag{3.20}
$$

where

$$
Z = \left[\frac{\gamma}{(L-s+1)} \frac{1}{P_h} \right]^{-\gamma} \left[\frac{1-\gamma}{(L-s+1)} \frac{1}{P_x} \right]^{\gamma-1}
$$

$$
\times \prod_{t=s}^{L} (1+r)^{(t-1)-1/(L-s+1)} \prod_{t=1}^{k-1} (H'_t - B_h)^{-\gamma/(L-s+1)}
$$

$$
\times \prod_{t=k}^{s-1} (\bar{H}'_t - B_h)^{-\gamma/(L-s+1)} \prod_{t=1}^{s-1} (X'_t - B_x)^{(\gamma-1)/(L-s+1)}
$$

An estimate of PVY' is obtained by substituting U'_1, the estimated level of utility attained given participation in year s for U_1 in equation (3.20):

$$
\text{PVY}'_1 = (U'_1)^{L/(L-s+1)} Z + Q \tag{3.21}
$$

3.4 Changes in consumption patterns

We are interested in determining how much more or less housing services are consumed by families participating in the programs in year s than would be consumed in the absence of the programs in year s.

Similarly, how much more or less nonhousing goods are consumed by families participating in the programs than would be consumed in their absence?

In the absence of the program in year s, the ith household would consume H''_{is} and X''_{is} in year s [see equations (3.14) and (3.15)]. Given participation, the family consumes \bar{H}'_{is} and X'_{is} [see equation (3.11)]. The proportional change in the ith family's consumption of housing services in year s, which results from its participation in a housing program in that year, is $(\bar{H}'_{is} - H''_{is})/H''_{is}$.[21]

These changes in consumption patterns can be compared to those that would result from an unrestricted cash grant of equal subsidy value. Ignoring administrative costs and inefficiency on the part of the government in producing housing services, the size of the subsidy to household i in year s, G_{is}, is the difference between the market rent of its subsidized unit and the rent the household is required to pay:

$$G_{is} = (P_{his}\bar{H}'_{is}) - (P'_{his}\bar{H}'_{is}) \tag{3.22}$$

If this subsidy were given to the household in the form of a cash grant instead of in the form of a housing program, it would add G_{is} to the household's income in year s. We can estimate H'''_{is} and X'''_{is}, the quantities of housing services and nonhousing goods consumed in the absence of the program in year s but in the presence of a cash grant equal to G_{is}, from equations (3.14) and (3.15):

$$H'''_{is} = H''_{is} + \frac{\gamma}{L-s+1}\frac{1}{P_h}G_{is} \tag{3.23}$$

$$X'''_{is} = X''_{is} + \frac{1-\gamma}{L-s+1}\frac{1}{P_x}G_{is} \tag{3.24}$$

Estimation procedures

In order to follow the steps outlined in Section 3.3 and arrive at an estimate of benefit, we must know or be able to estimate the following:

1. The life expectancy of the head of the household and the age at which he or she entered the workforce
2. The length of uninterrupted participation in a subsidized housing program
3. The real rate of interest
4. The prices of housing services and nonhousing goods over the household's planning horizon
5. Household income over the household's planning horizon
6. The rent of the subsidized housing unit, and the market rent of the subsidized housing occupied during the years of participation
7. The parameters of the utility function

The purpose of this chapter is to describe the procedures used to estimate these variables.

4.1 Length of life

As noted in Chapter 3, the model assumes that each household has a planning horizon equal to the remainder of the expected lifetime of the head of the household after entry into the workforce. In order to implement this model, it is assumed that all households have the same length of planning horizon, fifty-four years.[1] I arrive at this figure by assuming a common entry age of twenty-one and a common life expectancy of seventy-five.[2] Using the notation of Chapter 3, $L_i = 54$ for every household i. Excluded from the sample are all households with heads younger than twenty-one or older than seventy-four.

4.2 Length of participation
in a subsidized housing program

The model requires an estimate of the years of uninterrupted participation in a housing program. We also need an estimate of s_i and k_i, where s_i is defined as the year that 1977 represents in the planning horizon of the ith household and k_i is the year in its planning horizon in which the household moved into the subsidized housing unit.

Note that 1977 represents different points in different households' planning horizons depending on the age of the head of household in 1977. For example, 1977 represents year one for a person who is twenty-one and just entering the workforce. Alternatively, 1977 represents year 20 for someone who is forty and has been working for nineteen years. Thus,

$$s_i = \text{(age of head of } i\text{th household in 1977)} - 20$$

In the AHS, the statistics on age of head for those between twenty and seventy-five are classified into thirteen age brackets based on the age reported for the head as of his last birthday. In order to estimate s_i, a continuous age variable is approximated from this discontinuous data by setting age of head equal to the average age in each bracket.

The year in its planning horizon in which the ith household moved into its current subsidized housing unit, k_i, is estimated in the following way:[3]

$$k_i = s_i - \text{(length of tenure }_i + 1)$$

Length of tenure in a housing unit is calculated using data contained in the AHS on the year the head of household moved into his current housing unit. For those who moved into their present units in 1970 or after, the data report the actual year the head moved in. Thus, if the head of household moved into the subsidized unit in 1977, length of tenure is set equal to 1. If the head moved into the unit in 1976, length of tenure is set equal to 2, and so forth. However, for those who moved into their present units before 1970, the data report only whether they moved in between 1965 and 1970, between 1960 and 1964, between 1950 and 1959, or before 1950. For these households, length of tenure in the housing program is approximated by assuming that the household moved into the unit in the average year in each category. For 1949 or earlier, length of tenure is approximated to be thirty years.[4]

4.3 The real rate of interest

In order to calculate present values, future payments and receipts must be discounted by the real rate of interest. The real rate of interest can be defined as the premium commanded in the market by current real claims over future real claims. According to Fisherian interest theory, nominal or money rates of interest differ from real rates because of expected future rates of inflation. From Fisher's theory

$$R_t = r^* + \Pi_t + r^* \, \Pi_t$$

where R_t is the nominal rate of interest in period t; r^* is the expected real rate of interest, assumed to be constant over time and equal to the long-run or natural real rate of interest; and Π_t is the expected rate of inflation in period t. The relationship between real and nominal interest rates is usually expressed without the cross-product term or simply as $R_t = r^* + \Pi_t$. The cross-product term can be ignored to a fair approximation when r^* and Π_t are small. Also, with continuously compounded interest the term drops out entirely. Thus, the shorter the compounding period, the more accurate it is to ignore the cross-product term (Hirshleifer 1980, p. 508).

Several studies have examined the effects of inflationary expectations on the nominal rates of interest on U.S. Treasury securities, chosen because of their low default risk (see, for example, Gibson 1972 and Yohe and Karnosky 1969). In these studies, the practical problem is to find a measure of inflationary expectations. In a recent study, Vito Tanzi (1980) estimates the relationship between nominal interest rates and inflationary expectations using interest data on six-month and twelve-month U.S. Treasury securities and six alternative measures of inflationary expectations developed by Gibson (1972), Lahiri (1976), Frankel (1975), and Turnovsky (1970). The period covered for six-month Treasury bills is June 1959 to December 1975 and for twelve-month Treasury bills is June 1952 to December 1975.

Tanzi estimates an equation of the following form for each of the alternative measures of inflationary expectations:

$$R_t = a + b \, \Pi_t$$

On the assumption that the real rate of interest was constant over this period, the fitted parameter, a, is an estimate of the real rate of interest.

Tanzi's estimates for a vary depending on the measure of inflationary expectations used. The average estimate for real rate of interest on twelve-month bills is 3.47. The estimate from the equation that Tanzi suggests fits the data best is 2.71. The coefficients of the expectations

variables are all significantly less than one. Tanzi contends this may be due to misspecification or the fact that not all the effects of inflationary expectations are incorporated in the nominal interest rate.

Tanzi also tests the hypothesis that cyclical fluctuations can affect the nominal rate of interest and the expected real rate of interest. Formalizing his theory,

$$R_t = r^n + b\Pi_t + \theta(Y - \bar{Y})_t, \theta > 0$$

where r^n is the natural or long-run real rate of interest; Y is actual output; and \bar{Y} is potential or full employment output. This model retains the basic Fisherian theory in terms of inflationary expectations but relaxes the constraint of a constant real rate of interest by adding the level of economic activity as an explanatory variable. The addition of the measure of economic activity improves all of the equations. The coefficients of the expectations variables increase significantly and are in most cases close to one. The estimates of r^n for twelve-month bills using the various measures of inflationary expectations average 3.20, with 2.91 corresponding to Tanzi's best-fitting equation.

In this study, I assume that the real rate of interest is constant at 3 percent. This is in line with Tanzi's estimates of r^n but does not allow for variation of the real rate of interest over the business cycle.

4.4 Relative prices

The AHS contains no data on prices of housing services and nonhousing goods. I use the Bureau of Labor Statistics' (BLS) intermediate budget supplemented by the Urban Institute's place-to-place, constant-quality indexes of the price of housing as sources for relative prices.[5]

BLS price data have been used extensively in housing demand studies.[6] However, there are several problems associated with using BLS prices in the present study. First, the BLS prices are for metropolitan areas and for regions. Ideally, the model requires observations on prices faced by individual households. Using group mean prices in the model, instead of separate prices for each household (which are unavailable), results in misspecification of the demand equations (see Polinsky 1977 and Polinsky and Ellwood 1979).

A second problem arises from using the BLS budget data as a source of relative prices. The BLS budgets are designed to reflect cost-of-living differences among different areas for three income levels. The market baskets, which are priced in the different areas to obtain the budget estimates, are not identical from city to city. Area differences in the

costs of the market basket can be attributed to differences in quantities as well as differences in prices. The BLS points out:

Among the major components of the budgets, the comparisons for food at home, shelter, transportation, and clothing are for an equivalent, not an identical, list of goods and services. Thus, for these components both the quantities and prices may vary from city to city. . . . Area differences in the costs of all components other than food at home, shelter, transportation, and clothing are attributable to price differences, because within each budget the items and quantities priced were the same from place to place. (U.S. Department of Labor 1967, pp. 28–31)

For determining renter costs for the low- and middle-income groups, the standard housing unit is defined as follows:

Unfurnished five-room unit (house or apartment) in sound condition; [with] a complete private bath, a fully equipped kitchen; hot and cold running water; electricity, central or other installed heating; access to public transportation; schools, grocery stores, play space for children and location in residential neighborhood free from hazards or nuisances. (U.S. Department of Labor 1967, p. 42)

Gillingham (1975) has pointed out the subjective nature of this and similar definitions used in defining the BLS standard market basket. This subjectivity in the definition of a standard rental housing unit causes difficulties in holding qualities constant across cities. For example, it is questionable that "location in residential neighborhood free from hazards or nuisances" is held constant from city to city since it is not objectively defined in the budget standards.

A third criticism of BLS prices is that the pricing of the BLS standard market basket took place in 1967. Since then the BLS prices have been updated using various components of the Consumer Price Index (CPI) for each SMSA in the BLS sample. For example, the price of rental housing is updated using the rent component of the CPI. If the CPI is inaccurate, the updated BLS prices are incorrect.

Partly in response to criticism of the BLS prices, the Urban Institute has constructed new constant-quality, cross-sectional indexes of the price of housing. These indexes are calculated using AHS SMSA data for thirty-nine large SMSAs in 1974 and 1975. The technique used is the method of hedonic indexes.

With the hedonic technique, a housing unit is viewed as a bundle comprised of many housing characteristics, for example, number of rooms and type of heating system.[7] Each characteristic is assumed to have its own price that can be estimated with regression analysis. Given estimates of these characteristic prices for each of the thirty-nine SMSAs in the sample, the indexes of housing rents are calculated in

the following way. A particular bundle of housing characteristics for rental units is specified and then priced in each SMSA. The predicted rent for each SMSA can be taken as an estimate of the price per unit of housing services in that SMSA.

This hedonic technique is consistent with the method used to construct the BLS rental prices. With the BLS method, a particular housing bundle is specified. A sample of rental units within an SMSA with these particular characteristics is selected and the average rent of these units is calculated. This procedure is repeated in each SMSA using the same set of housing characteristics. The average rent of these units for each SMSA can be viewed as an estimate of the price per unit of housing services in that SMSA.

It is more likely that constant housing quality across SMSAs is maintained by the Urban Institute than by the BLS because many more housing characteristics are held constant. Furthermore, the bundle pricing underlying the Urban Institute's prices is more recent (1974 and 1975) than the bundle pricing underlying the BLS prices (1967). For these reasons, in this study Urban Institute prices are used in place of BLS prices when they are available.

A final practical problem with regard to estimating relative prices results from trying to match household data from the national AHS to available BLS and Urban Institute prices. The national AHS household data identify four census regions, each of the 125 SMSAs with 250,000 or more population at the time of the 1970 census, and metropolitan and nonmetropolitan residence. If a household is not located in one of the identification SMSAs, then urban or rural residence is also identified.[8]

The BLS price data are reported for 40 large and small SMSAs (some of which are not identified in the AHS) and for four regional nonmetropolitan areas. The Urban Institute prices are available only for 39 of the 125 large SMSAs identified by the AHS.

Since Urban Institute prices for nonhousing goods are unavailable, I rely solely on the BLS for these prices. I assign prices of nonhousing goods to the households in the following manner. (Appendix A lists the assigned prices of nonhousing goods by SMSA and region.) If the household is located in one of the 125 SMSAs identified in the AHS and in one of the 40 SMSAs included in the BLS data, then it is assigned the BLS price for that SMSA. If the household is located in one of the 125 SMSAs identified in the AHS but not in one of the 40 SMSAs included in the BLS data, it is assigned the BLS weighted average SMSA price for its census region. This average is computed by weighting the SMSA prices in the region by the population weights

reported by the BLS.[9] If the household is located in a nonmetropolitan or rural area, it is assigned its regional nonmetropolitan price reported by the BLS. Nonhousing price indexes are then constructed by dividing the assigned price for each household by the U.S. urban average price for nonhousing goods for 1976 reported by the BLS.

For housing prices, BLS prices are combined with Urban Institute prices. The BLS prices are in autumn 1976 dollars and the Urban Institute prices are in March 1975 dollars. The Urban Institute prices are updated to autumn 1976 using the rent component of the CPI.[10]

Even though the Urban Institute prices are based on a housing bundle specification that is consistent with the housing bundle specification used by the BLS, one still cannot be sure that housing quality is, in fact, held constant across SMSAs because the bundle specification used by the Urban Institute is more extensive than that used by the BLS. However, it is reasonable to conclude that substituting Urban Institute prices wherever possible will reduce the errors due to the variations in housing quality that exist in the BLS units.

Furthermore, I account for differences in the level of the two rent series by adjusting the Urban Institute prices in the following way. There are eighteen SMSAs that are contained in both the BLS and Urban Institute samples. The Urban Institute price is higher than the BLS price for fifteen of these SMSAs. I weight the BLS and the Urban Institute housing prices for these eighteen SMSAs by the number of year-round occupied housing units in the particular SMSA divided by the total number of year-round occupied housing units in all eighteen SMSAs (U.S. Department of Commerce 1977 and 1980, Table A.1). I compute the mean weighted BLS price and the mean weighted Urban Institute price for the eighteen SMSAs. The ratio of the mean weighted BLS price to the mean weighted Urban Institute price is the adjustment factor, which is applied to all the Urban Institute prices in order to adjust for differences in the level of prices between the two price sources. The adjustment factor is 0.85.

I assign housing prices to individual households in the AHS sample as follows. (Appendix A lists the assigned prices of housing services by SMSA and region.) If the household is located in one of the 125 large SMSAs identified in the AHS data and in one of the 39 SMSAs included in the Urban Institute sample, it is assigned the adjusted Urban Institute price for that SMSA. If the household is located in one of the 125 large SMSAs identified by the AHS but not in one of the 39 SMSAs identified by the Urban Institute, it is assigned either the BLS price for that SMSA if there is one or the weighted, adjusted average Urban Institute SMSA price for its census region. This average is computed by weighting the

adjusted Urban Institute SMSA prices in each region by the number of year-round occupied housing units in each SMSA divided by the total number of occupied housing units in the Urban Institute sample in the region.

If a household is located in a small or moderate size SMSA (and hence not identified in the AHS data), it is assigned the weighted average BLS SMSA price for its census region. This average is computed from the BLS prices by weighting the SMSA prices in the region by the population weights reported by the BLS. If the household is located in a nonmetropolitan or rural area, it is assigned its regional nonmetropolitan price reported by the BLS. Housing price indexes are then constructed by dividing the assigned price for each household by the U.S. urban average price for rental housing for 1976 reported by the BLS.

4.5 Household income

The model assumes that households equate their consumption expenditures and income receipts, not necessarily in any one period, but over their entire planning horizons. Thus, the model requires an estimate of household income for the fifty-four years of each household's planning horizon.

Since the model assumes that households make decisions regarding current expenditures based on current income and on expectations of future income, a measure of annual income is needed that excludes unexpected, short-run fluctuations in income. The purpose of this section is to describe the techniques used to estimate each household's stream of expected income over its planning horizon.

Several different methods have been used to exclude unexpected, short-run fluctuations in income from housing demand studies. The methods include income averaging, grouping of observations, using lagged or future income, and using a priori estimates of expected income.[11] Income averaging involves using a weighted or unweighted average of income over several periods under the assumption that transitory components average out over time (see, for example, Carliner 1973). Grouping involves the use of aggregated data based on the assumption that transitory income components will average out for the group (see, for example, DeLeeuw 1971). Lagged or future income is used as an instrumental variable for expected income on the assumption that lagged or future measured income is directly correlated with the expected component of current income but not correlated with the transitory component of current income (see, for example, Lee 1968).

The fourth method, a priori estimation, involves regressing current income on those household characteristics presumed to determine it. The estimated regression equation is then used to estimate expected income. This method has been used to estimate one year's expected income for households in Struyk's (1976) study of homeownership and Mayo's (1976) study of housing allowances. In this study, I use this method to estimate an income-generating function for each of four types of households using the 1977 data. The estimated regression equations are used to determine expected income for each household in every year of its planned horizon. These annual estimates of expected income are combined with estimates of the exogeneous growth rate of income to generate an income stream for every household over its planning horizon. The remainder of this section deals with the details of this procedure and the resulting income estimates.

Specification of variables and functional form

In choosing the household characteristics that are expected to determine household expected income, I rely on human capital theory. The narrow human capital theory states that an individual's current gross real earnings can be related to his or her past investments in human capital. That is,

$$Y_t = Y_0 + r_c \sum_{i=1}^{t-1} C_i$$

where Y_t is annual income of an individual in year t; Y_0 is income that would be earned in the absence of human capital investment; r_c is the average rate of return on human capital investments, assumed to be constant over time; and C_i is the cost of human capital investment in year i. Becker and Chiswick (1966) and Mincer (1974) have developed models that explain individual income as a function of human capital investments in the form of number of years of schooling and on-the-job training. In their models, years of experience and years of experience squared are used as a proxy for on-the-job training, which is assumed to decline linearly with time.

Various forms of their models are widely used in the literature to investigate income distributions and wage discrimination. These models, with some refinement, are useful for my purpose because the human capital theory on which they are based is essentially an expected income theory (Rosen 1977, p. 4). Unlike stochastic earnings theory, which assumes that earnings are a function of chance, human capital theory suggests that income can be explained by an individual's

investment in education and training, which add to the individual's ability to earn income.[12]

I expand the narrow human capital models in two ways. First, within the narrow human capital models no significant role is given to demographic variables. However, factors such as sex, marital status, and residence may help explain household income. Second, I assume that *household* income can be explained by the household *head's* investment in education and training and by certain other characteristics of the household. Therefore, I include other characteristics of the head and of the household in addition to education and experience of the head as explanatory variables.

The sample is divided into four household types by race and participation in a subsidized housing program. Separate income-generating functions are estimated for households of each type. The sample is stratified by race of head of household because of the possibility that whites and nonwhites face different prices in the labor market.[13] The sample is stratified by participation in a subsidized housing program to account for the possibility that living in subsidized housing affects work incentives because the subsidy decreases with increases in household income.

The dependent variable is the natural log of annual household income from all sources in 1977. Studies by Hechman and Polachek (1974) and Welland (1978) provide strong empirical support for the use of the natural log of income as the appropriate dependent variable in income-generating functions. Furthermore, their evidence suggests the semilogarithmic specification of the income function is superior to the double logarithmic and linear functional forms.

The following list contains the broad classes of independent variables included in the income model: (1) education of head of household, (2) experience of head, (3) sex of head, (4) marital status of head, (5) size and composition of the household, (6) sources of household income, and (7) location of the household. Several require further discussion.

Education of head of household: The statistics refer to the highest grade of school completed, not to the highest grade attended. School refers to formal education obtained in graded public or private schools, colleges, universities, or professional schools. Education received in vocational, trade, or business schools or noncredit adult education classes is not counted.

Experience of head of household: As noted above, the basic human capital models include years of experience and years of experience

squared as a proxy for on-the-job training. The Annual Housing Survey contains no data on years of experience. Several human capital studies have found age to be an adequate measure of experience (see, for example, Blinder 1974 and 1976). In this model, I use age and age squared as a measure of work experience.

In the Annual Housing Survey the statistics on age of head for those between twenty and seventy-five are classified into thirteen age categories based on the age reported for the head as of his last birthday. For the income model, a continuous age variable is approximated from this discontinuous data according to the procedure described in Section 4.2.

Underlying the income model is the assumption that differences in household income are attributable, at least partially, to differences in the productivity and labor force participation of the head. Consequently, several income studies include occupation of the head and current employment status of the head as independent variables (see, for example, Oaxaca 1973 and Struyk 1976). The AHS does not contain data on occupations. However, it does include data on whether the head of the household had a job the week before the AHS interview. This information is included in the present model as a measure of labor force participation of the head.

Size and composition of the household: Education, age, sex, marital status, and employment status are all defined in terms of the household head's status, while the dependent variable is household income. However, it is entirely possible that other household members contribute to household income. For example, other members of the family may work. Similarly, a household with a retired member may receive pension income or a household with dependent children may receive child support income. Furthermore, the composition of the household may have an effect on the ability and incentives of the members of the household to work. For example, the presence of young children may have a significant effect on the work histories of women. In this model size of the household as well as proportion of the household younger than six years old, proportion of the household between the ages of six and seventeen, and proportion of the household older than sixty-five are included as explanatory variables.

Sources of household income: The sources of household income may also significantly affect the incentives of members of the household to work. For example, recipients of welfare income may have diminished incentives to work because size of welfare payments is tied to wage and

salary income. Similarly, social security recipients are penalized for working under certain circumstances. In this model the proportions of total family income from various sources are included as explanatory variables to account for the effect of differences in income source mix on household income.

Location of the household: Several location and place size variables are included in the model to account for the effect of differences in residence on household income. Dummy variables account for census region of residence and residence in a large SMSA (population greater than 250,000), residence in an identified central city of a large SMSA, residence in a medium or small SMSA (population of 50,000 to 250,000), residence in a nonmetropolitan area (population of 2,500 to 49,999), or residence in a rural area (population less than 2,500).[14]

Estimated income model

Table 4.1 contains the definitions of the regressors included in the permanent income equations. The estimated regression equations explaining the natural log of household income for 1977 are presented in Table 4.2. The proportion of explained variance ranges from 39 percent for unsubsidized white households to 61 percent for subsidized nonwhite households. The constant term contains the effects of membership in the excluded categories. That is, the head is an unmarried, white male. The household lives in the West in a large SMSA, but not in an identified central city of a large SMSA. The household is composed entirely of people between the ages of eighteen and sixty-four and receives all of its income from the "other" income category.

All but one of the variables are significant in at least one of the equations and most enter with the expected sign. REGNE is insignificant in all four equations although it has a *t* statistic greater than one for every household type other than subsidized white renters.

The results indicate that, on average, holding other factors constant:

1. Higher levels of education lead to higher incomes.
2. For white and nonwhite unsubsidized households, those with older household heads, presumed to have more experience, have higher incomes, and the effect of experience on income declines over time. For subsidized households, AGEHD and AGEHDSQ have the expected signs but are insignificant.
3. HEADJOB is positive in all four equations and significant for every household type except subsidized white households.

TABLE 4.1

DEFINITION OF TERMS USED IN INCOME REGRESSIONS

Regressors	Description of Regressors
EDUCHD	Education of the head.
AGEHD	Age of the head.
AGEHDSQ	Age of head squared.
HEADJOB	1 if head had job last week; 0 otherwise.
SEXHD	Sex of head (1 if female; 0 if male).
MARRIED	Marital status of head. (1 if married; 0 if widowed, divorced, separated or never married.)
HHSIZE	Number of household members.
HHSIZESQ	Number of household members squared.
PROP6	Proportion of the household younger than 6 years old.
PROP617	Proportion of the household between the ages of 6 and 17.
PROP65	Proportion of the household older than 65 years old.

(PROP6 = PROP617 = PROP65 = 0 if the household is comprised entirely of members between the ages of 18 and 64.)

PROPEARN	Proportion of total household income from wages and salaries and net farm and nonfarm self-employment income.
PROPWELF	Proportion of total household income from welfare and public assistance income.
PROPUNEM	Proportion of total household income from unemployment compensation.
PROPWC	Proportion of total household income from workmen's compensation.
PROPALIM	Proportion of total household income from alimony and child support income.
PROPPENS	Proportion of total household income from social security pensions, private pensions and government employee pensions including railroad retirement income.
PROPDRI	Proportion of total household income from dividends, interest or rental income.

(PROPEARN = PROPWELF = PROPUNEM = PROPWC = PROPALIM = PROPPENS = PROPDRI = 0 if all household income comes from other sources not listed above, for example, veterans income, contributions, scholarships and insurance payments.)

REGNE	1 if household located in Northeast; 0 otherwise.
REGNC	1 if household located in Northcentral; 0 otherwise.
REGS	1 if household located in South; 0 otherwise.

(REGNE = REGNC = REGS = 0 if household located in West.)

TABLE 4.1--Continued

Regressors	Description of Regressors
CENCITY	1 if located in an identified central city of a large SMSA; 0 otherwise.
MEDSMSA	1 if located in medium or small SMSA; 0 otherwise.
NONMETRO	1 if located in a nonmetropolitan area; 0 otherwise.
RURAL	1 if located in rural area; 0 otherwise.

(CENCITY = MEDSMSA = NONMETRO = RURAL = 0 if located in large SMSA but not in its central city or its central city is not identified.)

TABLE 4.2

ESTIMATED RELATIONSHIPS BETWEEN NATURAL LOG OF 1977 TOTAL HOUSEHOLD
INCOME AND HOUSEHOLD CHARACTERISTICS BY HOUSEHOLD TYPES

Regressors	Unsubsidized		Subsidized	
	White	Nonwhite	White	Nonwhite
EDUCHD	.0595	.0431	.0033	.0193
	(26.16)	(7.70)	(4.16)	(2.33)
AGEHD	.0438	.0188	.0109	.00003
	(10.61)	(1.96)	(.73)	(.002)
AGEHDSQ	−.0004	−.0002	−.0002	−.0001
	(8.35)	(1.41)	(.92)	(.60)
HEADJOB	.1845	.1913	.1151	.1853
	(7.80)	(3.65)	(1.33)	(2.54)
SEXHD	−.2204	−.2413	−.2252	−.2600
	(10.80)	(5.31)	(2.58)	(2.98)
MARRIED	.0942	.1472	.0693	.0817
	(3.79)	(2.85)	(.66)	(.84)
HHSIZE	.2548	.1831	.2462	.2630
	(11.97)	(5.84)	(3.25)	(5.28)
HHSIZESQ	−.0180	−.0088	−.0166	−.0144
	(8.88)	(3.40)	(2.40)	(2.93)
PROP6	−.6960	−.3967	−.8291	−1.0577
	(11.03)	(3.28)	(3.77)	(5.77)
PROP617	−.4631	−.1553	−.1700	−.7152
	(7.66)	(1.50)	(.85)	(5.21)

TABLE 4.2--Continued

| | Unsubsidized | | Subsidized | |
| | White | Nonwhite | White | Nonwhite |
Regressors				
PROP65	.2298	.2625	.1478	.3048
	(4.84)	(2.42)	(1.09)	(2.19)
PROPEARN	.7684	.6650	.1461	.4075
	(13.25)	(5.70)	(.76)	(1.91)
PROPWELF	-.1116	-.2188	-.6555	-.2222
	(1.62)	(1.84)	(3.46)	(1.05)
PROPUNEM	-.6441	-.1958	-.4591	-.6388
	(5.42)	(.83)	(1.00)	(2.10)
PROPWC	.4782	-.2446	.2905	.5932
	(2.96)	(.46)	(.58)	(1.52)
PROPALIM	.0372	.3203	-.8914	-.1799
	(.32)	(1.05)	(2.99)	(.44)
PROPPENS	.0890	-.0997	-.3983	-.2768
	(1.36)	(.79)	(2.07)	(1.28)
PROPDRI	.1258	-1.7980	.3683	2.43
	(1.52)	(3.57)	(.96)	(4.97)
REGNE	.0231	-.0817	.0203	-.0849
	(1.12)	(1.36)	(.29)	(1.06)
REGNC	-.0045	-.1207	.0040	-.1649
	(.23)	(2.33)	(.05)	(2.26)
REGS	-.0657	-.2734	-.0671	-.4353
	(3.54)	(5.79)	(1.03)	(6.36)
CENCITY	-.0456	-.0244	.0576	.1427
	(2.65)	(.66)	(.91)	(2.66)
MEDSMSA	-.0608	-.1055	.0569	-.1329
	(2.56)	(1.72)	(.73)	(1.71)
NONMETRO	-.1178	-.2046	-.0145	.1937
	(5.41)	(3.30)	(.23)	(2.38)
RURAL	-.1434	-.3316	.0091	.1525
	(7.35)	(5.56)	(.12)	(1.46)
CONSTANT	6.4036	7.2400	7.9366	8.1828
\bar{R}^2	.39	.48	.50	.61
STD. ERROR OF ESTIMATE	.6194	.6439	.5833	.4631
NUMBER OF OBSERVATIONS	8574	1731	663	453

Note: t statistics in parentheses.

4. Female-headed households earn less income than male-headed households for each household type.
5. For unsubsidized households, those with married heads earn more income than those with unmarried heads. Marital status is insignificant for subsidized households.
6. As the number of household members increases, household income increases but at a declining rate.
7. As the proportion of children in the family increases, household income decreases. As the proportion of family members over sixty-five increases, household income increases.
8. As the proportion of earned income increases, household income increases, while as the proportion of income from welfare and unemployment compensation increases, household income falls. PROPWC is significant only for unsubsidized white households. PROPPENS and PROPALIM are significant only for subsidized white renters. PROPDRI is negative and significant for unsubsidized nonwhite households and positive and significant for subsidized nonwhite households.
9. The effects of the locational variables differ across the four household types. Generally, households located in the North-central region or the South earn less income relative to those located in the West. Households residing in medium to small SMSAs or in rural areas earn less income relative to those living in large SMSAs. NONMETRO has a significant negative effect on income for unsubsidized households. However, NONMETRO is positive and significant for subsidized, nonwhite households. The effect of living in an identified central city of a large SMSA is negative and significant for unsubsidized white renters and positive and significant for subsidized nonwhite renters.

Lifetime expected income

Given the estimated regression equations, the next step is to calculate expected income over the fifty-four years of each household's planning horizon. Income-generating functions are formed for each household type from the estimated regression equations shown in Table 4.2. An estimate of the natural log of expected income for years 1 through 54 is calculated by inserting each household's values for its independent variables into the appropriate function for households of its type, holding all the variables constant at their 1977 levels except age of head, which varies from twenty-one to seventy-four. Taking the antiloga-

rithm of these estimates for every year $t = 1, \ldots, 54$ results in estimates of annual household expected income over the entire planning horizon of the household.

These estimates account for changes in income due to changes in the head's experience and seniority over the household's planning horizon, but do not account for other changes in household characteristics that occur over time or for exogenous changes in income resulting from growth of the economy. Clearly, other variables besides age of the head can change over the household's planning horizon. It is certainly plausible to expect, for example, that size, composition, and even location of the household will change as the years go by. However, incorporating different demographic histories for each household type into the predictions of expected income is beyond the scope of this study and remains an area for future research.

In order to account for exogenous changes in income resulting from growth of the economy, I assume that households plan to share in this growth (see Miller 1965). The estimates of income are adjusted by the geometric average rate of change in output per person-hour in the nonfarm business sector of the economy over the period 1948 to 1978 (Council of Economic Advisors 1979, Table B-38, p. 277).

The final formula for estimating the present value in year 1 of each household's stream of expected income is

$$P\hat{V}Y_1 = \sum_{t=1}^{54} \frac{(\hat{Y}_t)(1 + g)^{t-s-1}}{(1 + r)^{t-1}}$$

where g is the average change in output per person-hour, calculated to be 0.019; r is the real rate of interest, assumed equal to 0.03 (see Section 4.3); and s is age of head of household in 1977 minus 20 (see Section 4.2).

4.6 Rents and quantities of subsidized housing

The model requires estimates of the subsidized and market rents of the housing units occupied by participating families during the years they have lived in subsidized housing. The subsidized rent for 1977, year s, is contained in the data. Subsidized rents for previous years of participation, k through $s - 1$, must be estimated.

Tenant rents in federally subsidized housing programs typically vary according to household income and size. Assume that the ratio of subsidized rent to expected household income for every participating family is constant over the years of participation. This rent-to-income ratio can be determined by dividing the 1977 subsidized rent contained

in the data by predicted expected income for 1977 (see Section 4.6). This ratio, when multiplied by predicted income for previous years of participation, results in estimates of subsidized rents for years k through $s - 1$. Thus

$$\text{Subsidized rent}_t = \left[\frac{\text{Subsidized rent}_s}{\text{Predicted income}_s} \right] [\text{Predicted income}_t]$$

for years $t = k, \ldots, s - 1$.

To determine quantities of subsidized housing services consumed by participating families, market rent of each household's subsidized housing unit is estimated and divided by the market price index of housing services, P_h. In equation form for every household i

$$H'_i = \text{Market rent}_i / P_{hi}$$

where H'_i is the quantity of housing services contained in the subsidized unit occupied by household i.

Market rents are estimated using hedonic pricing techniques. These techniques have been used extensively in the housing literature to investigate racial discrimination in housing markets, to estimate the effect on market rents and sale prices of different housing characteristics, and to estimate housing price indexes, as well as to estimate rents of subsidized housing units.[15]

In this study, rents of unsubsidized housing units are regressed on a set of housing characteristics. The estimated coefficients are used to estimate the market rents of subsidized units with similar characteristics. The estimated market rents are then divided by the relevant market price index of housing (see Section 4.4) to arrive at estimates of the quantities of housing services consumed by participating households in 1977. It is assumed that these quantities have not changed over the years of each household's participation.

Rent estimation model

In order to estimate the market rent of a subsidized housing unit in 1977, it is assumed that the market rent of a subsidized unit is equal to the average rent of unsubsidized units with the same characteristics. Specifically, the model assumes that the rent of an unsubsidized housing unit is an additive function of the stochastic regressors described in Table 4.3 and an error term with mean zero that is independent of the regressors.

The dependent variable is monthly gross rent, where gross rent is computed in the Annual Housing Survey in the following way:

TABLE 4.3

DEFINITION OF TERMS USED IN RENT REGRESSIONS

Regressors	Description of Regressors
AGEBLDG	Age of unit.
AGEBLDGSQ	Age of unit squared.
ROOMS	Number of rooms.
ROOMSQ	Number of rooms squared.
BEDRMS	Number of bedrooms.
BATH1.5	1 if unit has one and a half bathrooms; 0 otherwise.
BATH2	1 if unit has two bathrooms; 0 otherwise.
MT2BATH	1 if unit has more than 2 bathrooms; 0 otherwise.
POORBATH	1 if unit has no bathroom or shares a bathroom; 0 otherwise.

(BATH1.5 = BATH2 = MT2BATH = POORBATH = 0 if unit has one bath.)

ELEV	1 if building has elevator; 0 otherwise.
OUTLETS	1 if working electrical outlets not present in each room; 0 otherwise.
PRIVACY	1 if must pass through bedroom to get to other room; 0 otherwise.
COOKFUEL	1 if primary cooking fuel is electricity; 0 otherwise.
AIRCOND	1 if unit has air conditioning; 0 otherwise.
TYPEAIR	1 if unit has central air conditioning; 0 if unit has room units or no air conditioning.
OWNER	1 if owner lives on property; 0 otherwise.
CENTRAL	1 if unit has central warm air furnace; 0 otherwise.
STEAM	1 if unit has steam or hot water heat; 0 otherwise.
BADHEAT	1 if unit has room heaters without flue, fireplaces, stove, or no heating equipment; 0 otherwise.

(CENTRAL = STEAM = BADHEAT = 0 if unit has heat pump, built-in electric units, floor or wall furnace, or room heaters with flue.)

UNIT3	1 if building has 3-9 units; 0 otherwise.
UNIT4	1 if building has 10-49 units; 0 otherwise.
UNIT5	1 if building has more than 50 units; 0 otherwise.

(UNIT3 = UNIT4 = UNIT5 if building has less than 3 units.)

FLOOR2	1 if 4-6 floors in building; 0 otherwise.
FLOOR3	1 if 7-12 floors in building; 0 otherwise.

TABLE 4.3--Continued

Regressors	Description of Regressors
FLOOR4	1 if 13 or more floors in building; 0 otherwise.
(FLOOR2 = FLOOR3 = FLOOR4 = 0 if building has 1-3 floors.)	
NGHD	1 if respondent's overall opinion of neighborhood according to street conditions and available neighborhood services is excellent; 0 otherwise.
ABANHSG	1 if interviewer observes abandoned housing on street; 0 otherwise.
REGNE	1 if unit located in Northeast; 0 otherwise.
REGNC	1 if unit located in Northcentral; 0 otherwise.
REGS	1 if unit located in South; 0 otherwise.
(REGNE = REGNC = REGS = 0 if unit located in West.)	
MEDSMSA	1 if unit located in medium or small SMSA; 0 otherwise.
NONMETRO	1 if unit located in nonmetropolitan area; 0 otherwise.
RURAL	1 if unit located in rural area; 0 otherwise.
(MEDSMSA = NONMETRO = RURAL = 0 if unit located in large SMSA.)	

"Gross rent" is the contract rent plus the estimated average monthly cost of utilities (electricity, gas, water) and fuels (oil, coal, kerosene, wood, etc.) if these items are paid for by the renter (or paid for him by someone else . . .) in addition to rent. Contract rent is the monthly rent agreed to, or contracted for, regardless of any furnishing, utilities, or services that may be included. Thus, gross rent is intended to eliminate differentials which result from varying practices with respect to the inclusion of utilities and fuel as part of the rental payment. (U.S. Department of Housing and Urban Development 1979a, pp. 35-6)

The sample used to estimate the market rent equations includes all unsubsidized, private, unfurnished rental units for which all the necessary data are reported.[16] The sample is stratified by race, and separate market rent equations are estimated for whites and nonwhites because of the possibility that they face different housing prices. Initially, the ordinary least-squares (OLS) estimation procedure is used. The estimated OLS market rent equations for whites and nonwhites are reported in columns 1 and 3 of Table 4.4.

TABLE 4.4

ESTIMATED RELATIONSHIPS BETWEEN MONTHLY GROSS RENT AND HOUSING UNIT
CHARACTERISTICS BY RACE--ORDINARY AND WEIGHTED LEAST-SQUARES RESULTS

| Regressors | White | | Nonwhite | |
	OLS (1)	WLS[a] (2)	OLS (3)	WLS[a] (4)
AGEBLDG	-2.41 (7.74)	-2.68 (9.91)	.41 (.54)	1.15 (1.45)
AGEBLDGSQ	.01 (2.35)	.02 (3.82)	-.03 (1.80)	-.04 (2.63)
ROOMS	16.89 (6.12)	6.78 (-)[b]	21.64 (3.62)	12.70 (-)[b]
ROOMSQ	-.52 (2.21)	.61 (2.23)	-1.01 (1.77)	.22 (.32)
BEDRMS	10.44 (6.31)	9.92 (5.71)	10.70 (3.23)	7.63 (1.98)
BATH1.5	39.34 (12.93)	25.35 (12.28)	25.93 (3.71)	25.35 (2.75)
BATH2	62.97 (20.42)	61.11 (17.60)	40.62 (5.35)	41.53 (4.06)
MT2BATH	161.12 (12.69)	161.97 (16.01)	197.28 (9.55)	184.09 (5.81)
POORBATH	-26.99 (4.96)	-35.44 (8.12)	-22.32 (3.36)	-17.58 (2.85)
ELEV	14.04 (1.31)	5.68 (.79)	42.04 (2.56)	7.73 (.57)
OUTLETS	-12.25 (2.82)	-13.57 (3.11)	-9.61 (1.66)	-11.09 (1.77)
PRIVACY	-10.72 (3.86)	-6.13 (2.62)	-2.78 (.64)	-1.58 (.38)
COOKFUEL	-1.75 (1.06)	-4.53 (3.08)	9.61 (2.52)	3.09 (.82)
AIRCOND	7.40 (3.99)	6.93 (4.13)	21.68 (5.43)	23.03 (5.49)
TYPEAIR	8.85 (3.20)	7.34 (3.05)	15.53 (2.27)	20.64 (2.86)
OWNER	-9.11 (3.71)	-4.92 (2.28)	-4.80 (.84)	-4.81 (.82)
CENTRAL	16.04 (7.76)	13.17 (6.98)	21.84 (4.56)	20.95 (3.88)
STEAM	24.88 (9.94)	16.34 (7.79)	37.20 (6.49)	23.25 (4.05)
BADHEAT	-23.87 (7.67)	-18.54 (6.62)	-8.89 (1.83)	-5.47 (1.10)

TABLE 4.4—Continued

	White		Nonwhite	
	OLS	WLS[a]	OLS	WLS[a]
Regressors	(1)	(2)	(3)	(4)
UNIT3	−7.25	−1.90	−1.42	7.06
	(3.43)	(1.00)	(.33)	(1.57)
UNIT4	−9.11	−2.79	8.11	14.45
	(3.32)	(1.20)	(1.37)	(2.45)
UNIT5	−1.82	−.48	27.46	29.35
	(.34)	(.13)	(2.28)	(3.05)
FLOOR2	18.37	29.11	11.85	12.07
	(2.04)	(4.50)	(.92)	(1.05)
FLOOR3	45.08	35.42	−53.18	−2.64
	(3.55)	(4.42)	(2.40)	(.15)
FLOOR4	93.30	73.65	−.12	34.95
	(7.26)	(8.95)	(0)	(1.76)
NGHD	6.88	9.39	16.16	10.05
	(4.06)	(6.36)	(3.55)	(2.02)
ABANHSG	−14.45	−10.36	−3.41	−4.57
	(4.43)	(3.44)	(.94)	(1.25)
REGNE	2.67	3.01	−18.61	−20.08
	(1.02)	(1.38)	(2.74)	(2.94)
REGNC	−25.37	−22.33	−54.71	−52.36
	(10.55)	(10.58)	(9.20)	(8.63)
REGS	−34.27	−31.26	−58.20	−59.11
	(14.40)	(14.66)	(11.72)	(12.13)
MEDSMSA	−10.87	−8.24	−6.94	−3.18
	(4.16)	(3.48)	(1.19)	(.48)
NONMETRO	−22.69	−24.70	−2.166	−14.88
	(9.10)	(10.61)	(3.70)	(2.46)
RURAL	−37.96	−29.94	−30.86	−26.85
	(16.36)	(13.16)	(5.03)	(4.23)
CONSTANT	180.61 (−)[b]	201.36 (34.00)	111.00 (−)[b]	122.64 (7.94)
\bar{R}^2	.52	.66	.54	.56
STD. ERROR OF ESTIMATE	62.39	14.98	56.19	16.02
NUMBER OF OBSERVATIONS	7129	7129	1503	1503

NOTE: *t* statistics in parentheses

[a]Weighted by number of rooms

[b]The SPSS regression package does not report standard errors for the constant term (see Nie 1975).

King and Mieszkowski (1973) and Grether and Mieszkowski (1974) found evidence of heteroskedasticity in their hedonic pricing models, with increased variation in the disturbance term associated with size of housing units. In these studies, as well as in Olsen and Barton (1983), each observation is divided by a measure of size of housing unit (either area in square feet or number of rooms). Based on this evidence, I suspected that number of rooms might be a source of heteroskedasticity in the market rent models.

I tested for the possibility that the disturbance variance increases with the square of rooms using the F test suggested by Goldfeld and Quandt (1965). In order to perform the test, the observations for both the white and nonwhite samples are ordered in accordance with number of rooms. For both samples four-room housing units are omitted, and separate rent regressions are fitted by ordinary least squares using observations on housing units with three or fewer rooms and on housing units with five or more rooms.[17] Let SSE_1 denote the sum of squared residuals from the regression using observations on housing units with five or more rooms and SSE_2 denote the sum of squared residuals from the regression using observations on housing units with three or fewer rooms. According to Goldfeld and Quandt the statistic

$$\frac{\dfrac{SSE_1}{T_1 - p}}{\dfrac{SSE_2}{T_2 - p}}$$

will, on the assumption of homoskedasticity, have the F distribution with $(T_1 - p, T_2 - p)$ degrees of freedom, where T_1 and T_2 are the number of observations in the large and small housing unit samples, respectively, and p is the number of explanatory variables in the model.

The test results for the white and nonwhite rent equations are presented in Table 4.5. In both cases the null hypothesis, homoskedasticity, is rejected at the 1 percent level of significance.

To correct for heteroskedasticity, each observation is divided by number of rooms, thus transforming the dependent variable to rent per room, and weighted least-squares (WLS) regressions are run for the white and nonwhite samples. The WLS results are reported in columns 2 and 4 of Table 4.4. The WLS coefficients are used to estimate monthly gross rent per room of each subsidized housing unit. Annual market rent of the subsidized housing units is then calculated by multiplying predicted monthly gross rent per room by 12 and by the number of rooms in the unit.

TABLE 4.5

HOMOSKEDASTICITY TEST

Rent Equation	F Statistic	Degrees of Freedom
White	2.953	(2,890; 1,732)
Nonwhite	1.413	(409; 487)

In the WLS models for nonwhites and whites most variables are significant or have a t statistic greater than one and enter with the expected sign. Exceptions include presence of an elevator (ELEV), which is an important explanatory variable in the OLS models but becomes insignificant in the WLS rent models. It was expected that presence of the owner on the property (OWNER) would tend to increase rents because of the possibility that owner residence results in better maintenance of the building and improved tenant behavior. However, the coefficient for OWNER is negative in both the white and nonwhite rent equations (although OWNER is insignificant in the nonwhite models).

Several differences in signs, relative magnitudes, and significance levels of estimated coefficients between the white and nonwhite WLS rent models also emerge. I expected a negative relationship between rent per room and age of building, indicating that older buildings rent for less. This was the case for the white sample up to a building age of sixty-seven years. For nonwhites the coefficients for AGEBLDG and AGEBLDGSQ indicate a positive relationship between rent per room and age of building up to a building age of fourteen years.

ROOMSQ, PRIVACY, FLOOR3, and MEDSMSA are significant in the white WLS equation but not in the nonwhite equation. Electricity as the primary cooking fuel (COOKFUEL) tends to decrease the rents charged white households and increase the rents charged nonwhite households (although COOKFUEL is insignificant in the nonwhite WLS model).

Number of units in the building (UNIT3, UNIT4, UNIT5) leads to very different results in the white and nonwhite models. Relative to buildings with less than three units, living in buildings with more units tends to decrease rents for white households and increase rents for nonwhite households, everything else held constant.

Similarly, the results indicate that, on average, holding other factors constant, whites living in the Northeast pay higher rents relative to those living in the West, while nonwhites in the Northeast pay lower rents relative to those living in the West.

On examining these WLS results it is important to note that the housing characteristics included in the models do not include all the variables that might influence rent. If the omitted variables are correlated with the included variables, the effects of the excluded variables will be reflected in the estimated coefficients of the included variables.

Furthermore, these estimated rent equations are used to predict market rents of subsidized housing units. Since the housing characteristics included in the models are not exhaustive, subsidized housing units that are the same as unsubsidized units with respect to the included characteristics may be different with respect to the omitted characteristics. As a result, the predicted rents will be biased, although the direction of the bias is unclear.

4.7 The parameters of the utility function

In Section 3.2 the expenditure equations for housing services for nonparticipating households are derived by maximizing the utility function (3.1) subject to the constraint (3.2). Assuming that all nonparticipating households have identical parameters, B_h, B_x, and γ, the housing expenditure equation (3.3) can be respecified:

$$P_{hi}H_{it} = B_h P_{hi} + \frac{\gamma(1+r)^{t-1}}{54}\left[\sum_{t=1}^{54} \frac{Y_{it} - B_h P_{hi} - B_x P_{xi}}{(1+r)^{t-1}}\right]$$

for every t. Nonlinear least-squares estimation would yield consistent estimators of the parameters.[18]

The assumption of identical tastes across households is restrictive. Following Olsen and Barton (1983), the assumption is relaxed, at least partially, and differing tastes are allowed for in two ways. First, the sample is stratified by dividing nonparticipating households into sixteen types by race, region, and household size. Second, all households of the same type are assumed to have the same displacement parameters, B_h and B_x, but different parameters, γ_i. Let γ be the mean of γ_i for all households of a particular type. Then for any household i within this type, $\gamma_i = \gamma + v_i$ where $E(v_i) = 0$. Note, the parameters B_h, B_x, and γ may be different for households of different types.

Given these assumptions, housing expenditure equations for nonparticipating households of a particular type can be respecified and estimated by nonlinear least squares:

$$P_{hi}H_{it} = B_h P_{hi} + \frac{\gamma(1+r)^{t-1}}{54}\left[\sum_{t=1}^{54}\frac{Y_{it} - B_h P_{hi} - B_x P_{xi}}{(1+r)^{t-1}}\right] + u_i$$

where

$$u_i = v_i\left[\frac{(1+r)^{t-1}}{54}\left(\sum_{t=1}^{54}\frac{Y_{it} - B_h P_{hi} - B_x P_{xi}}{(1+r)^{t-1}}\right)\right]$$

The parameters are estimated using 1977 data for a random sample of nonparticipating households of each type. Thus, P_{hi}, H_i, P_{xi}, Y_i, in addition to v_i, are random variables. Assume that P_{hi}, P_{xi}, Y_i, and v_i are independent. This implies that P_{hi}, P_{xi}, Y_i, and u_i are uncorrelated and that nonlinear least-squares estimators of B_h, B_x, and γ are consistent.

The introduction of the random coefficient γ_i results in heteroskedasticity and a loss of efficiency of the estimates of the parameters (Theil 1971, pp. 622–8). The gain from the random coefficient model is the partial relaxation of the assumption of identical tastes across households. The large size of many of the samples reduces the impact from the loss of efficiency.

Table 4.6 contains the unconstrained nonlinear least-squares estimates of the parameters for participating households. These estimates for participating households are based on the stratified sample of nonparticipating households for which all the necessary information is reported. Applying these estimates of the parameters to participating households of the same type may result in sample selection bias in the estimates of the parameter γ for participating households if the tastes of participating households differ systematically from the tastes of nonparticipating households (see Heckman 1979).[19] The expected direction and extent of the bias, however, are not clear.

It has been argued, for example, that although all families eligible for participation in a housing program would receive some benefit from participation (possibly negative), it is the families with the largest benefits who participate. Since the housing programs distort consumption toward housing, the families receiving the largest benefits are those with the strongest tastes for housing and thus the largest marginal propensity to spend on housing γ_i. Consequently, the mean of this parameter, γ, for participating families is greater than its mean for nonparticipating families and the estimate of γ using a sample of nonparticipating families will be too low.

One problem with this argument is that it does not account for the fact that not every household that applies for admittance to a housing program is accepted. Criteria for acceptance differ among programs

and localities, and local housing authorities are frequently directed to give special consideration to households living in the worst unsubsidized housing. If households living in the worst housing get in first, then participating families might have weaker tastes for housing, on average, relative to all eligible households. In this case, the estimate of γ using a sample of nonparticipating families will be too high.[20]

Previous housing studies have been subject to this type of sample selection bias. Olsen and Bierman (1982) evaluate the importance of this bias in their measurement of the benefits of public housing using a procedure described by Heckman (1979). They find that accounting for selection bias has little effect on their results (their estimate of mean benefit changes by less than 5 percent). Methods for detecting and correcting sample selection bias remain an important area for research. The purpose of this research is to improve the methodology of benefit–cost analysis along different lines, and so I ignore this problem.

An additional consideration regarding these parameter estimates is that the utility function (3.1) is undefined when $H_{it} < B_h$ or $X_{it} < B_x$. Therefore it is desirable to constrain the parameters to satisfy these inequalities. I see no way of doing this for B_x because I have no estimate of X_{it}. However, H_{it} can be estimated by dividing estimated annual market rent for participating households (see Section 4.6) by the price of a unit of housing services:

$$H_{it} = \text{annual market rent}_{it}/P_{hi}$$

I constrain B_h to be less than the estimated minimum value of H_{it} for participating households of a particular type.[21] For example, the minimum quantity of housing services consumed in 1977 by white, participating, one- or two-member households living in the Northeast is 1,265.08. I constrain B_h to be less than this, thereby ensuring that $H_{it} > B_h$ for all households of that type. When this constraint is entered, the estimates of B_h are always at their boundary values. For example, when B_h is constrained to be less than 1,265.08, the estimate of B_h that results is 1,265.00. Thus, the practical result of constraining B_h to be less than H_{it} is that B_h is set equal to the minimum value of H_{it} of participating households of particular types.

Table 4.7 contains the constrained estimates of the parameters based on the sample of nonparticipating households for which all the necessary information is reported. I apply the constrained estimates of the parameters to participating households of the same type in order to estimate the benefits reported in Chapter 5. Note that the constrained estimates of B_h and B_x are lower than the unconstrained estimates, although the constrained estimates of γ are higher.

TABLE 4.6

UNCONSTRAINED ESTIMATES OF THE PARAMETERS OF THE UTILITY FUNCTION BY HOUSEHOLD TYPE
(Asymptotic t statistics in parentheses)

Race	Region	Household Size	B_h	B_x	Y	R^2	Number of Cases
White	Northeast	1-2	1384 (18.66)	-1801 (4.19)	.086 (15.93)	.89	1104
		3-	1869 (14.18)	-541 (.34)	.076 (7.93)	.85	593
	Northcentral	1-2	1318 (18.93)	-1246 (3.59)	.095 (19.27)	.89	1462
		3-	1535 (11.96)	-2956 (1.84)	.083 (9.81)	.86	769
	South	1-2	1623 (20.55)	-1089 (2.66)	.088 (15.75)	.87	1540
		3-	1632 (13.79)	1368 (1.83)	.116 (15.51)	.86	1050
	West	1-2	1682 (23.01)	-815 (1.43)	.074 (12.35)	.88	1351
		3-	1594 (13.50)	-5896 (2.89)	.079 (9.06)	.86	758

64

Nonwhite						
Northeast	1-2	1555 (3.77)	1705 (.92)	.138 (2.83)	.66	118
	3-	1074 (3.48)	-12820 (2.00)	.086 (3.28)	.87	88
Northcentral	1-2	1781 (14.33)	1988 (1.60)	.068 (5.07)	.92	227
	3-	2026 (12.72)	-7446 (1.22)	.031 (2.45)	.93	151
South	1-2	1613 (16.46)	2062 (3.51)	.105 (8.32)	.90	444
	3-	1876 (16.54)	3815 (3.37)	.086 (7.61)	.87	439
West	1-2	1439 (8.81)	302 (.32)	.115 (6.70)	.91	168
	3-	1675 (8.52)	-4144 (.84)	.057 (3.26)	.91	118

TABLE 4.7

CONSTRAINED ESTIMATES OF THE PARAMETERS OF THE UTILITY FUNCTION BY HOUSEHOLD TYPE
(Asymptotic t statistics in parentheses)

Race	Region	Household Size	B_h	B_x	Y	R^2	Number of Cases
White	Northeast	1-2	1265 (16.97)	-2104 (5.23)	.093 (17.15)	.89	1104
		3-	1432 (10.72)	-2940 (2.02)	.092 (9.54)	.85	593
	Northcentral	1-2	1271 (18.24)	-1344 (3.97)	.098 (19.90)	.89	1462
		3-	1535 (11.96)	-2956 (1.84)	.083 (9.81)	.86	769
	South	1-2	1211 (15.00)	-1820 (5.55)	.111 (19.56)	.87	1540
		3-	1412 (11.86)	651 (.92)	.125 (16.67)	.86	1050
	West	1-2	714 (8.95)	-2586 (7.40)	.136 (20.85)	.87	1351
		3-	1139 (9.50)	-8007 (4.28)	.095 (10.75)	.86	758

Nonwhite

Northeast	1–2	1432 (3.45)	1266 (.77)	.148 (3.01)	.66	118
	3–	1074 (3.48)	−12821 (2.00)	.086 (3.28)	.87	88
Northcentral	1–2	1520 (12.05)	246 (.29)	.088 (6.46)	.91	227
	3–	1735 (10.75)	−11101 (2.00)	.041 (3.15)	.92	151
South	1–2	1349 (13.42)	939 (2.53)	.132 (10.28)	.89	444
	3–	1331 (11.28)	424 (.54)	.117 (10.10)	.87	439
West	1–2	1439 (8.81)	302 (.32)	.115 (6.70)	.91	168
	3–	1395 (7.03)	−7213 (1.49)	.066 (3.73)	.90	118

An additional result of using the constrained parameter estimates is that it lessens the number of participating households who must be deleted from the sample because their permanent incomes are insufficient to pay the expected tenant rents of their subsidized units, to purchase the subsistence quantities of housing services for the years they do not plan to be in subsidized housing, and to purchase the subsistence quantities of nonhousing goods for their entire planning horizons. This could occur because permanent income is underestimated or because the true displacement parameters for these households are below the mean for their group. In any case, the utility function is undefined for these households.

Using the unconstrained parameter estimates 183 households, 16 percent of the sample of subsidized households, must be deleted because of insufficient permanent income to estimate benefits. The households omitted tend to be those with lower current household income and are overwhelmingly nonwhite (162 households or 92 percent), female-headed (152 households or 83 percent), public housing residents (152 households or 83 percent), and live in the South (145 households or 79 percent). Omitting these households reduces the number of nonwhite households by 37 percent, female-headed households by 23 percent, and households living in the South by 33 percent.

With the constrained parameters listed in Table 4.7 the number of households that must be deleted due to insufficient wealth drops to 37, which represents only 3 percent of the sample of subsidized households.[22] These omitted households tend to have lower incomes, less education, older heads, and to be smaller than other participating households. Again, they are overwhelmingly nonwhite (34 households or 92 percent), female-headed (28 households or 76 percent), Southerners (33 households or 89 percent), and public housing residents (34 households or 92 percent).

The estimated parameters contained in Table 4.7 are satisfactory in many respects. The estimates of γ are all between 0 and 1. The estimates of B_h have the right sign and their relative magnitudes overall suggest that larger households have larger subsistence housing requirements.

I did not expect negative signs for the estimates of B_x, which are often interpreted as the subsistence levels of nonhousing goods. In judging the acceptability of the estimated parameters, however, it is useful to remember that they are estimated using a sample of households who for the most part have incomes nowhere near subsistence levels and who consume much more than subsistence levels of housing services and nonhousing goods. The estimated parameters may serve quite adequately for these types of households but not so well for

households with incomes close to subsistence. Furthermore, the estimated parameters determine the marginal rate of substitution between housing services and nonhousing goods for the sample households. Thus, although one would not expect, for example, a negative subsistence level for nonhousing goods, the estimated parameters do allow the marginal rate of substitution to be different than if the displacement parameters, B_h and B_x, were assumed restrictively to be zero (the assumption underlying the Cobb–Douglas utility function).[23]

CHAPTER 5

Empirical results

This chapter presents estimates of the effects of government-subsidized rental housing programs based on the model developed in Chapter 3, the variables as estimated by the procedures described in Chapter 4, and data contained in the 1977 Annual Housing Survey. In Section 5.1 the magnitude of benefits to participating families is investigated, and estimated changes in consumption patterns due to the subsidy programs are compared with consumption changes under a program of unrestricted cash grants. In Section 5.2 the distribution of benefits of the subsidy program is estimated. Section 5.3 compares these results to results of previous studies.

5.1 Changes in consumption patterns and magnitude of benefits to participating households

The model developed in Chapter 3 uses a Hicksian measure of consumer surplus to estimate the benefits of the programs to participating families. This involves selecting a utility function and comparing the utility surface attained under participation in the programs with the utility surfaces attained under certain alternatives to participation. Specifically, an inter-temporal, Stone–Geary utility function is chosen and consumption patterns are compared under the following policy alternatives: (1) the housing programs are terminated in the beginning of 1978; (2) the housing programs are terminated in the beginning of 1977; (3) the housing programs are terminated in the beginning of 1977 and replaced with a program of unrestricted cash grants which operates in 1977 only.

In this model, then, the measure of benefit from a housing program is the cash grant that enables a participating family to be as well off without participation in 1977 and future years as with participation in 1977, but in no future years. In other words, the benefit measure is the value a participating family places on one more year's operation of the housing program.

70

The Annual Housing Survey sample is the result of stratified random sampling. The AHS public-use data tape contains a set of sampling weights designed to make the AHS sample representative of the population as a whole. These sampling weights are used to compute all means reported. In addition, the AHS data allow me to separate public housing households from households participating in other subsidized housing programs. To facilitate comparison of my results with previous studies of this type, most of which concern only public housing, I report separately results for (1) the public housing program, (2) all other types of housing subsidies, and (3) all housing subsidy programs combined. I also report certain results by race of head of household.

Using equation (3.14), the annual housing expenditures of subsidized households in the absence of the programs (i.e., with early termination in the beginning of 1977) are estimated. The difference between this and the predicted market rent of the subsidized units in 1977 gives the change in consumption of housing goods in that year due to the operation of the programs for one more year. Using equations (3.11) and (3.15), I estimate the annual expenditures on nonhousing goods in 1977 under these programs and in their absence, respectively. The difference between the two is the change in the consumption of nonhousing goods in that year due to the operation of the programs for one more year. Note that allowing the programs to operate one more year has effects on future consumption of both goods as well as on current (1977) consumption. The effects on future consumption are investigated separately in this section.

As reported in Table 5.1, the results indicate that, in the aggregate, all subsidized households together consumed 40 percent more housing services and 1.7 percent more nonhousing goods in 1977 than they would have consumed in the absence of the programs. Separating public housing households from households receiving other housing subsidies, we find little difference in the effects of the programs. Public housing households, in the aggregate, consumed 41 percent more housing services in 1977 than they would have without the operation of the public housing program in that year. Households in other subsidized housing programs consumed 37 percent more housing services. Public housing households consumed 1.6 percent more nonhousing goods and households in other programs consumed 1.9 percent more nonhousing goods in 1977 than they would have in the absence of the programs.

The difference in changes in consumption of housing services between whites and nonwhites in all programs is more substantial. In the aggregate, white households increased consumption of housing services

TABLE 5.1

AGGREGATE EFFECTS OF GOVERNMENT-SUBSIDIZED HOUSING PROGRAMS (1977)

	All Subsidy Programs Combined	Low-Rent Public Housing	Other Subsidized Housing Programs	Whites-- All Programs	Nonwhites-- All Programs
Mean annual housing expenditure by subsidized families in absence of programs	$1,799	$1,798	$1,802	$1,748	$1,871
Mean annual market rent of their subsidized units	$2,519	$2,537	$2,473	$2,634	$2,359
Percentage increase in aggregate consumption of housing services by subsidized families	40.0%	41.1%	37.2%	50.7%	26.1%
Mean annual expenditure on other goods by subsidized families in absence of programs	$2,347	$2,441	$2,105	$2,293	$2,424
Mean annual expenditure on other goods by subsidized families under these programs	$2,387	$2,480	$2,145	$2,333	$2,464
Percentage increase in aggregate consumption of other goods	1.7%	1.6%	1.9%	1.7%	1.6%
Mean annual subsidized rent of participating families	$1,473	$1,401	$1,663	$1,586	$1,315
Percentage reduction in market price of housing services to subsidized families	-41.5%	-44.8%	-32.8%	-39.8%	-44.3%
Mean annual income	$6,742	$6,990	$6,098	$7,317	$5,937
Mean annual benefit	$ 633	$ 731	$ 379	$ 577	$ 712
Mean annual subsidy	$1,046	$1,136	$ 810	$1,048	$1,044
Number of households in sample	1,088	804	284	664	424
Number of households in population	1,747,933[a]	1,262,177[a]	485,754[a]	1,020,633	727,299

[a]These numbers are not equal to the numbers prepared by HUD (see Table 1.1). The discrepancies are the result of differences in the definition of occupied subsidized housing units used by HUD and the AHS. Additional differences can arise if subsidized housing residents either do not know or are embarrassed to tell the AHS interviewer that their unit is subsidized.

in 1977 by 51 percent relative to what they would have consumed in the absence of the programs, whereas nonwhite households increased consumption by 26 percent. Differences in the changes in consumption of nonhousing goods between whites and nonwhites are slight. Whites increased consumption of nonhousing goods in 1977 by 1.7 percent, and nonwhites increased consumption by 1.6 percent.

These results are aggregate effects. Of course, different households made different percentage changes in the consumption of housing services. Of all subsidized households, 11 percent occupied worse housing than they would have in the absence of the programs. Nine percent of public housing households occupied worse housing as a result of the program, and 17 percent of households in other subsidy programs occupied worse housing as a result of participation in 1977.

Using equation (3.18), the annual benefit of the subsidy programs in 1977 to each participating household is estimated. The mean value is reported in Table 5.1. For all subsidy programs combined, mean annual benefit is $633. From the viewpoint of the participating households, this is equivalent to a 9 percent increase in income.[1] For the public housing program taken separately, the mean annual benefit is $731 – equivalent, on average, to a 10 percent increase in income. The mean annual benefit from other subsidized housing programs is substantially less, $379. This is equivalent, on average, to a 6 percent increase in the income of participating families. For white households, the mean annual benefit is $577, representing an 8 percent increase in income; and for nonwhite households mean annual benefit is $712, representing a 12 percent increase in income.

The housing programs reduce the effective market price of housing services to subsidized households by a substantial amount on average: 42 percent to all subsidized households, 45 percent to public housing households, 33 percent to participants in other subsidized housing programs, 40 percent to white participating households, and 44 percent to nonwhite households. Comparing mean annual benefit to mean annual subsidy (computed as the difference between subsidized rent and predicted market rent and reported in Table 5.1) suggests that in all programs the subsidized households, both white and nonwhite, value this reduction in price at less than its cost to taxpayers.[2] The substantial difference between mean annual benefit and mean annual subsidy ($413 for the subsidy programs combined; $405 for public housing; and $431 for other subsidy programs) illustrates the distortion in 1977 in consumption patterns from the viewpoint of the participating households due to the in-kind nature of the housing subsidy system.

Replacing the operation of all subsidy programs in 1977 with unre-

stricted cash grants distributed in 1977 only and equal to the difference between the market and subsidized rent of the subsidized unit would increase aggregate benefits to participating households by 66 percent. Replacing the operation of the public housing program and other subsidized housing programs with such a cash grant program would increase aggregate benefits by 55 and 114 percent, respectively. Alternatively, by giving participating households unrestricted cash grants equal to the value they place on the subsidy program, it would be possible to induce the families to consume a combination of goods they consider as satisfactory as the combination consumed under the in-kind subsidy programs, while reducing taxpayer cost by at least 39 percent for all subsidy programs combined, 36 percent for public housing, and 53 percent for other subsidy programs.

It is likely that taxpayers as well as participating families benefit from the operation of the subsidy program. Although I am not able to estimate directly the value of these programs to taxpayers, I can investigate certain effects of the program upon which this value most likely depends. The traditional argument in support of housing subsidy programs implies that recipients consume more housing services and less nonhousing goods than they would choose if they were given unrestricted cash grants that allow them to consume any combination of the two goods with the same market value as the combination consumed under the programs. Table 5.2 presents some aggregate effects of replacing the operation of the subsidy programs in 1977 with unrestricted cash grants to be distributed in 1977 only, equal to the difference between the market and subsidized rents of the subsidized housing units.

In the aggregate, Table 5.2 shows that for 1977 all subsidy programs combined and the public housing programs and other subsidy programs taken separately have the desired effects with respect to both housing and nonhousing expenditures. Using equation (3.23), I estimate the annual housing expenditure in 1977 for each participating household, assuming each is given a cash grant in place of subsidized housing. The difference between this and the predicted market rent of the subsidized units in 1977 gives the change in the consumption of housing services that would occur if the subsidy programs were replaced with cash grants.

The results indicate that, in the aggregate, a one-year cash grant program would decrease housing consumption by 28 percent relative to consumption with the subsidy programs. Cash grants would decrease housing consumption for public housing households by 29 percent, and for households in other subsidy programs by 27 percent. Cash grants

TABLE 5.2

AGGREGATE EFFECTS OF REPLACING GOVERNMENT-SUBSIDIZED RENTAL HOUSING PROGRAMS WITH UNRESTRICTED CASH GRANTS (1977)

	All Subsidy Programs Combined	Low-Rent Public Housing	Other Subsidized Housing Programs	Whites— All Programs	Nonwhites— All Programs
Mean annual market rent of subsidized units	$2,519	$2,537	$2,473	$2,634	$2,359
Mean annual housing expenditure by subsidized families with cash grants in place of subsidized housing	$1,809	$1,808	$1,811	$1,760	$1,878
Percentage decrease in aggregate consumption of housing services with cash grants in place of subsidized housing	-28.2%	-28.7%	-26.8%	-33.2%	-20.4%
Mean annual expenditure on other goods by subsidized families under these programs	$2,387	$2,480	$2,145	$2,333	$2,464
Mean annual expenditure on other goods by subsidized households with cash grants in place of subsidized housing	$2,429	$2,525	$2,179	$2,392	$2,480
Percentage increase in aggregate consumption of other goods with cash grants in place of subsidized housing	1.8%	1.8%	1.6%	2.5%	0.6%
Mean annual subsidy (cash grant)	$1,046	$1,136	$ 810	$1,048	$1,044

would decrease housing consumption by whites 33 percent and by nonwhites 20 percent. For some individual households, however, cash grants would be more stimulative of housing consumption in 1977 than the subsidy programs. Eleven percent of all subsidized households, 9 percent of public housing households, and 17 percent of households participating in other subsidy programs would consume more housing with the cash grant than with the in-kind subsidy.

Using equations (3.11) and (3.24), I estimate the annual expenditure on nonhousing goods by each participating household given the operation of the subsidy programs in 1977, and alternatively with cash grants in their place. The difference between the two gives the change in consumption of nonhousing goods that would result if the subsidy programs were replaced in 1977 with cash grants. The results, reported in Table 5.2, indicate that in the aggregate, relative to the subsidy programs, cash grants would increase consumption of nonhousing goods by 1.8 percent for participants in all subsidy programs combined as well as in the public housing program. Participants in other subsidy programs would increase consumption of nonhousing goods by 1.6 percent if a one-year cash grant replaced the 1977 operation of the programs. Looking at participating households distinguished by race, we find that cash grants would result in white households increasing their consumption of nonhousing goods by 2.5 percent and nonwhite households by 0.6 percent.

The results reported so far have dealt with estimated changes in consumption patterns in 1977 only. However, the model developed in Chapter 3 assumes that households plan consumption decisions not only for the current year but for future years as well. It is assumed that subsidized households initially expect to be able to participate in the various subsidy programs through 1978. Future planned consumption of housing and nonhousing goods reflects this expectation. If the housing programs are terminated in 1977, one year early, or if the programs are replaced by a cash grant system, then the model allows for the possibility that future consumption plans will be altered.

Using equations (3.10), (3.11), (3.14), (3.15), (3.23), and (3.24), I estimate changes in planned consumption for future years with the housing programs, with cash grants, and with neither the housing programs nor cash grants. Tables 5.3 to 5.5 report aggregate future planned consumption effects one, two, five, and ten years after the current year, 1977. Row 4 in each of these tables is the percentage difference in housing services consumed with existing programs and with no subsidy whatsoever. Row 5 is percentage difference in consumption with the existing programs and with cash grants. The follow-

ing discussion refers to the effects of all housing subsidy programs combined (Table 5.3) since the results for all three groupings of subsidy programs (total, public housing, other subsidies) are almost identical.

The results show that the expectation of being able to participate in a subsidized housing program in 1977 tends to increase slightly planned consumption of housing services in future years, even though the programs are not available beyond 1977. These future consumption effects decline over time. For all subsidy programs combined (see Table 5.3) the planned consumption increases range from 0.28 percent in 1978 to 0.05 percent in 1987. If we replaced the subsidy programs with one-year cash grants, households would plan to consume yet a bit more housing in each of the future years (0.27 percent in 1978; 0.10 percent in 1987). Thus, the estimates in rows 4 and 5 of Table 5.3 show that although the subsidized housing programs are, in the aggregate, more stimulative of housing consumption than cash grants in the current year, cash grants are more stimulative of housing consumption in future years.

Overall, though, the results suggest that future planned consumption of housing services given participation in a housing subsidy program in 1977, given a cash grant in 1977, and given no program or cash grant, are quite similar. That is, once a household loses its in-kind housing subsidy, its planned future consumption of housing drops almost to the level the household would have planned if it had not participated in 1977 in the first place. If the household is given an unrestricted cash grant in 1977, planned future consumption of housing will be greater than planned consumption given the in-kind subsidy, but by only a small amount.

Turning to nonhousing goods, the results tell a different story. They indicate that both the subsidized housing programs and the cash grant program have larger effects on planned future consumption of nonhousing goods than on planned future consumption of housing services. For all housing subsidy programs combined, participation in 1977 increases planned consumption of nonhousing goods by 1.6 percent for 1978. By 1987 the increases decline to 0.3 percent. If the housing programs are replaced by a one-year cash grant, planned consumption of nonhousing goods is increased by an additional 1.6 percent in 1978, and this decreases to 0.4 percent in 1987. As in the case of housing services, we find that planned future consumption of nonhousing goods is stimulated more by a cash grant than by an in-kind subsidy. Furthermore, the results indicate that participation this year (1977) in either a housing subsidy program or a one-year cash grant

TABLE 5.3

AGGREGATE FUTURE CONSUMPTION EFFECTS OF SUBSIDIZED HOUSING PROGRAMS AND ALTERNATIVE POLICIES— HOUSEHOLDS IN ANY SUBSIDY PROGRAM

	Year s 1977	Year $s+1$ 1978	Year $s+2$ 1979	Year $s+5$ 1982	Year $s+10$ 1987
Mean annual housing expenditure by subsidized families in absence of subsidized housing programs in 1977	$1,799	$1,815	$1,832	$1,888	$1,994
Mean annual housing expenditure with subsidized housing programs operating in 1977	$2,519[a]	$1,820	$1,837	$1,890	$1,995
Mean annual housing expenditure with cash grants in place of subsidized housing in 1977	$1,809	$1,825	$1,841	$1,893	$1,997
Percentage change in aggregate consumption of housing services by subsidized families with the housing programs operating in 1977	40.0%	.28%	.27%	.10%	.05%
Percentage change in aggregate consumption of housing services with cash grants in place of subsidized housing in 1977	-28.2%	.27%	.22%	.16%	.10%

Mean annual expenditure on other goods in absence of subsidized housing programs in 1977	$2,347	$2,502	$2,661	$3,134	$4,055
Mean annual expenditure on other goods with subsidized housing programs operating in 1977	$2,387	$2,543	$2,704	$3,153	$4,066
Mean annual expenditure on other goods with cash grants in place of subsidized housing in 1977	$2,429	$2,583	$2,742	$3,175	$4,082
Percentage change in aggregate consumption of other goods with the housing programs operating in 1977	1.7%	1.6%	1.6%	0.6%	0.3%
Percentage change in aggregate consumption of other goods with cash grants in place of housing programs in 1977	1.8%	1.6%	1.4%	0.7%	0.4%
Number of households in sample	1,088	1,088	1,088	982	877
Number of households in population	1,747,933	1,747,933	1,747,933	1,559,920	1,395,011

[a]In 1977, with the subsidy programs operating, mean annual housing expenditure of subsidized families is mean annual market rent of their subsidized housing units.

TABLE 5.4

AGGREGATE FUTURE CONSUMPTION EFFECTS OF SUBSIDIZED HOUSING PROGRAMS AND ALTERNATIVE POLICIES—HOUSEHOLDS IN PUBLIC HOUSING

	Year s 1977	Year $s+1$ 1978	Year $s+2$ 1979	Year $s+5$ 1982	Year $s+10$ 1987
Mean annual housing expenditure by subsidized families in absence of subsidized housing programs in 1977	$1,798	$1,814	$1,831	$1,890	$1,997
Mean annual housing expenditure with subsidized housing programs operating in 1977	$2,537[a]	$1,819	$1,836	$1,892	$1,999
Mean annual housing expenditure with cash grants in place of subsidized housing in 1977	$1,809	$1,824	$1,841	$1,895	$2,001
Percentage change in aggregate consumption of housing services by subsidized families with the housing programs operating in 1977	41.1%	.28%	.27%	.11%	.10%
Percentage change in aggregate consumption of housing services with cash grants in place of subsidized housing in 1977	-28.1%	.27%	.27%	.16%	.10%

Mean annual expenditure on other goods in absence of subsidized housing programs in 1977	$2,441	$2,601	$2,767	$3,274	$4,227
Mean annual expenditure on other goods with subsidized housing programs operating in 1977	$2,480	$2,642	$2,808	$3,296	$4,241
Mean annual expenditure on other goods with cash grants in place of subsidized housing in 1977	$2,525	$2,685	$2,851	$3,317	$4,256
Percentage change in aggregate consumption of other goods with the housing programs operating in 1977	1.6%	1.6%	1.5%	0.7%	0.3%
Percentage change in aggregate consumption of other goods with cash grants in place of housing programs in 1977	1.8%	1.6%	1.5%	0.6%	0.4%
Number of households in sample	804	804	804	690	634
Number of households in population	1,262,177	1,262,177	1,262,177	1,140,582	1,027,563

[a] In 1977, with the subsidy programs operating, mean annual housing expenditure of subsidized families is mean annual market rent of their subsidized housing units.

TABLE 5.5

AGGREGATE FUTURE CONSUMPTION EFFECTS OF SUBSIDIZED HOUSING PROGRAMS AND ALTERNATIVE POLICIES—
HOUSEHOLDS IN OTHER SUBSIDY PROGRAMS

	Year s 1977	Year s+1 1978	Year s+2 1979	Year s+5 1982	Year s+10 1987
Mean annual housing expenditure by subsidized families in absence of subsidized housing programs in 1977	$1,802	$1,818	$1,833	$1,883	$1,983
Mean annual housing expenditure with subsidized housing programs operating in 1977	$2,473[a]	$1,823	$1,839	$1,884	$1,983
Mean annual housing expenditure with cash grants in place of subsidized housing in 1977	$1,811	$1,827	$1,842	$1,887	$1,986
Percentage change in aggregate consumption of housing services by subsidized families with the housing programs operating in 1977	37.2%	.28%	.33%	.05%	0%
Percentage change in aggregate consumption of housing services with cash grants in place of subsidized housing in 1977	-26.8%	.22%	.16%	.16%	.15%

Mean annual expenditure on other goods in absence of subsidized housing programs in 1977	$2,105	$2,244	$2,387	$2,752	$3,573
Mean annual expenditure on other goods with subsidized housing programs operating in 1977	$2,145	$2,286	$2,430	$2,765	$3,576
Mean annual expenditure on other goods with cash grants in place of subsidized housing in 1977	$2,179	$2,318	$2,461	$2,790	$3,596
Percentage change in aggregate consumption of other goods with the housing programs operating in 1977	1.9%	1.9%	1.8%	0.5%	0.1%
Percentage change in aggregate consumption of other goods with cash grants in place of housing programs in 1977	1.6%	1.4%	1.3%	0.9%	0.6%
Number of households in sample	284	284	284	170	114
Number of households in population	485,754	485,754	485,754	419,338	367,450

[a]In 1977, with the subsidy programs operating, mean annual housing expenditure of subsidized families is mean annual market rent of their subsidized housing units.

program has a larger effect on planned future consumption of non-housing goods than on planned future consumption of housing.

The value of the programs to taxpayers depends not only on the magnitude of benefits received by participating families and on resulting changes in consumption patterns but also on the distribution of the benefits of the subsidy programs. Section 5.2 investigates the welfare distributional effects of the housing subsidy programs.

5.2 Distribution of benefits

Table 5.6 compares average household characteristics of all subsidized households, public housing households, and households in other subsidy programs to the population of U.S. households. Comparing column 1 with column 4, we find that subsidized households as a group are quite different from all U.S. households. Not holding other characteristics constant, subsidized households, on average, earn substantially less income and have younger household heads. In addition, subsidized households are more likely to have a nonwhite or female head and to live in the South or the West, and less likely to live in the Northcentral region than the average U.S. household.

There are also noticeable differences between characteristics of public housing households (column 2) and households participating in other subsidy programs (column 3). Public housing households have higher incomes and larger families, and are younger than other subsidized households. Public housing households are also more likely to have nonwhite or female heads and live in the South and less likely to live in the West than other subsidized households.

Cross tabulations of benefits provide an additional way to analyze the distribution of benefits to participating families. Tables 5.7 to 5.9 present distributions of benefits by income class controlling for household size for all subsidy programs combined. The distributions for public housing and other subsidy programs are presented in Appendix B. Sampling weights are used to compute the percentages reported in these tables.

The cross tabulations for all subsidy programs combined provide moderate support for the conclusion that benefit decreases as income of participating families rises. Specifically, for one- to two-person households Table 5.7 reports that 16 percent of the lowest income households (income < $4,000) receive minimum benefit (< $200) while 67 percent of the highest income households (income ≥ $12,000) receive minimum benefit. Also, 21 percent of the poorest households receive maximum benefit (≥ $1,400) while only 5 percent of the highest in-

TABLE 5.6

COMPARISON OF CHARACTERISTICS OF FAMILIES IN ALL SUBSIDY PROGRAMS COMBINED,
LOW-RENT PUBLIC HOUSING, AND OTHER SUBSIDIZED HOUSING
PROGRAMS TO THE POPULATION OF U.S. HOUSEHOLDS (1977)

	All Subsidy Programs Combined	Low-Rent Public Housing	Other Subsidized Housing Programs	U.S. Households[a]
Mean annual income	$6,742	$6,990	$6,098	$16,000
Mean number of persons in household	2.95	3.15	2.45	2.81
Median age of head	42	37	47	47
Median years of education of head	12	12	12	13
Percentage of households headed by nonwhite	42	45	34	12
Percentage of households headed by female	58	60	51	25
Percentage of households living in Northeast	21	21	20	23
Percentage of households living in Northcentral	21	21	22	27
Percentage of households living in South	35	40	23	32
Percentage of households living in West	23	19	35	19
Number of households in sample	1,088	804	284	
Number of households in population	1,747,933[b]	1,262,177[b]	485,754[b]	76,030,000

[a]From U.S. Department of Commerce (1978 and 1979c).

[b]These numbers are taken from the AHS and do not correspond to the numbers prepared by HUD (see Table 1.1) because of definitional differences and reporting errors.

come households receive maximum benefit. For three- to four-person households (Table 5.8), 23 percent of the poorest households receive minimum benefit and 25 percent of the poorest households receive maximum benefit. However, 57 percent of the highest income households receive minimum benefit and only 1 percent receive maximum

TABLE 5.7

DISTRIBUTION OF BENEFITS BY INCOME CLASS FOR ONE- TO TWO-PERSON HOUSEHOLDS IN ALL
SUBSIDY PROGRAMS COMBINED (Sample Sizes in Parentheses)

Benefit Class	<$4,000	Income Class $4,000-7,999	$8,000-11,999	≥$12,000	Population Percentages (Sample Size)
<$200	16% (44)	29% (40)	32% (17)	67% (28)	25% (129)
$200-599	7% (18)	16% (22)	37% (20)	21% (9)	14% (69)
$600-999	22% (59)	23% (32)	22% (12)	2% (1)	20% (104)
$1,000-1,399	35% (96)	23% (32)	6% (3)	5% (2)	26% (133)
≥$1,400	21% (58)	9% (13)	4% (2)	5% (2)	15% (75)
Population Percentage (Sample Size)	54% (275)	27% (139)	11% (54)	8% (42)	100% (510)

TABLE 5.8

DISTRIBUTION OF BENEFITS BY INCOME CLASS FOR THREE- TO FOUR-PERSON HOUSEHOLDS IN ALL
SUBSIDY PROGRAMS COMBINED (Sample Sizes in Parentheses)

Benefit Class	<$4,000	Income Class $4,000-7,999	$8,000-11,999	≥$12,000	Population Percentage (Sample Size)
<$200	23% (26)	28% (29)	46% (39)	57% (43)	36% (137)
$200-599	12% (14)	17% (17)	24% (20)	28% (21)	19% (72)
$600-999	18% (21)	24% (25)	13% (11)	8% (6)	17% (63)
$1,000-1,399	22% (25)	13% (13)	9% (8)	5% (4)	13% (50)
≥$1,400	25% (18)	18% (19)	8% (7)	1% (1)	15% (55)
Population Percentage (Sample Size)	30% (114)	27% (103)	23% (85)	20% (75)	100% (377)

TABLE 5.9

DISTRIBUTION OF BENEFITS BY INCOME CLASS FOR FIVE OR MORE PERSON HOUSEHOLDS
IN ALL SUBSIDY PROGRAMS COMBINED (Sample Sizes in Parentheses)

Benefit Class	<$4,000	Income Class $4,000-7,999	$8,000-11,999	>$12,000	Population Percentage (Sample Size)
<$200	22% (11)	10% (8)	28% (11)	31% (10)	20% (40)
$200-599	14% (7)	13% (10)	28% (11)	22% (7)	17% (35)
$600-999	26% (13)	18% (14)	18% (7)	19% (6)	20% (40)
$1,000-1,399	28% (14)	26% (20)	18% (7)	19% (6)	23% (47)
>$1,400	12% (6)	33% (26)	10% (4)	9% (3)	19% (39)
Population Percentage (Sample Size)	25% (51)	39% (78)	20% (40)	16% (32)	100% (201)

benefit. For households with five or more members (Table 5.9), 22 percent of the poorest households receive minimum benefit and only 12 percent receive maximum benefit. For the highest income families, however, 31 percent receive minimum benefit while 9 percent receive maximum benefit.

The regressions reported in Table 5.10 summarize the distributive effects of the combined housing subsidy programs, public housing taken separately, and other housing subsidy programs. In order to account for the fact that the AHS data are collected from both high- and low-cost areas, I deflate nominal benefits and income using a cost-of-living index for autumn 1977, constructed from Department of Labor data (1977, Tables 24 and 25) as the ratio of the Consumer Price Index (CPI) for each area to the CPI in Atlanta, Georgia. These adjustments being made, I regress real annual benefit on real annual income and the other household characteristics listed in Table 5.10.

The coefficients of the equations indicate how real benefit varies with household characteristics. The standard errors and coefficients of

TABLE 5.10

DISTRIBUTIVE EFFECTS OF GOVERNMENT-SUBSIDIZED RENTAL HOUSING PROGRAMS

Dependent Variable – Annual Real Benefit

Household Characteristics	Households in Any Subsidy Program	Public Housing Households	Households in Other Subsidized Housing Programs
Annual real income in thousands	-26.73 (5.97)	-39.21 (9.24)	12.95 (1.06)
Race of head (1 if nonwhite; 0 otherwise)	81.28 (1.53)	-3.08 (.059)	110.69 (.855)
Sex of head (1 if female; 0 otherwise)	130.85 (2.45)	120.17 (2.29)	103.77 (.791)
Age of head in years	12.33 (7.29)	11.49 (6.87)	11.16 (2.77)
Education of head in years	-27.12 (3.33)	-26.16 (3.29)	-36.57 (1.85)
Household size	59.65 (4.05)	74.36 (5.26)	-43.79 (1.104)
Region of residence: Northeast (1 if NE; 0 otherwise)	-109.78 (1.47)	-175.38 (2.32)	-147.03 (.877)
Northcentral (1 if NC; 0 otherwise)	-209.55 (-2.88)	-310.15 (4.20)	-59.58 (.717)
South (1 if South; 0 otherwise) (NE=NC=S=0 if West)	-221.15 (3.25)	-385.08 (5.68)	35.17 (.214)
Place size:			
MEDSMSA (1 if small or medium SMSA; 0 otherwise)	-112.89 (1.51)	-131.98 (1.84)	-101.27 (.532)
Nonmetro (1 if nonmetropolitan area; 0 otherwise)	-123.27 (1.81)	-120.28 (1.86)	-317.95 (1.73)
Rural (1 if rural area; 0 otherwise)	-58.41 (.72)	-57.29 (.75)	-265.57 (1.19)
(MEDSMSA=Nonmetro=Rural=0 if large SMSA)			
Constant	461.72	783.21	278.10
\overline{R}^2	.18	.30	.08
Standard error	769.52	645.09	947.59
Mean real benefit	627	723	379
Number of observations	1088	804	284

NOTE: t statistics in parentheses.

determination indicate the variability of real benefits among similarly situated households. An important difference between the information contained in the regression equations and that presented in Table 5.6 is that the regression equations show how benefit varies with one household characteristic, when other characteristics are held constant. Other characteristics are not held constant in Table 5.6.

For all subsidized households the results indicate strongly that, on average, real benefits are greater for poorer and larger households and for households with older, female, or less educated heads. In addition, the results clearly show that benefits are lower for families living in the Northcentral and South relative to families living in the West. The relationships between annual real benefit and race of head and place size are weaker, as indicated by the low t statistics. The results suggest, somewhat tentatively, that nonwhites receive larger real benefits than whites and families living in the Northeast receive smaller real benefits than families living in the West. Families living in small or medium SMSAs, nonmetropolitan or rural areas, all receive smaller real benefits than families residing in large SMSAs.

For public housing households the results are similar for the most part. The only dramatic change occurs for race of head. For public housing households the results indicate that race is not significant in explaining variations in real benefits.

For the sample of households that receive other subsidies the regression results are quite different. Most of the variables are insignificant in that equation. In fact, age of head, education of head, and location in a nonmetropolitan area are the only household characteristics that remain significant in explaining the variation in real benefits among participants in housing programs other than public housing.

The small coefficients of determination and large standard errors of all three regression equations indicate that there is enormous variation in real benefits among households that are the same with respect to the twelve household characteristics listed. In other words, there is not equal treatment of equals among subsidized households. One explanation is that there are large differences in the attractiveness of the housing units contained in a single program and in the different programs. Among households that are similar with respect to the twelve characteristics, some will occupy new units in excellent condition while others will occupy older units in poor condition, and in most programs the tenant's rent does not depend on the attractiveness of the unit.

Also, it is important to note that there has been a trend in subsidized housing toward building projects exclusively for the elderly. For example, 61 percent of the public housing and Section 8 new construc-

TABLE 5.11

DIFFERENCES IN ESTIMATED REAL BENEFIT BETWEEN HOUSEHOLDS ONE STANDARD DEVIATION
ABOVE AND BELOW THE MEAN VALUE OF EXPLANATORY VARIABLE

Explanatory Variable	Differences in Real Benefit		
	Households in Any Subsidy Program	Public Housing Households	Households in Other Subsidized Housing Programs
Annual real income in thousands	$160	$244	$ 68
Age of head	$213	$193	$203
Education of head	$ 94	$ 88	$133
Household size	$112	$142	$ 73

tion and substantial rehabilitation units approved for construction, under construction, or construction completed in 1977 were reserved for elderly households (HUD 1978, Tables 91 and 114). Thus, the typical household headed by an older person lives in newer housing than other households, which is why a positive relationship between real benefit and age of head is not unexpected.

Table 5.11 contains differences in estimated real benefit (predicted from the regression equations of Table 5.10) between those households one standard deviation above and below the mean value of annual real income, age, and education of the head, and household size. The results indicate that for all households combined and public housing households the greatest differences in real benefit occur between households with real income or age of head one standard deviation greater and smaller than the mean. For households in other subsidy programs the greatest differences in real benefit are seen between households one standard deviation above and below the mean values of age and education of the head.

Regressions for subsidized households including real income, age of head, education of head, and household size squared as explanatory variables are also estimated. In general, the consistency of the coefficient signs across the three equations (Table 5.12) suggests nonlinearities in the relationships between real benefit and household characteristics. Annual real benefit is determined to fall at a decreasing rate as

TABLE 5.12

ADDITIONAL BENEFIT REGRESSIONS

Household Characteristics	Dependent Variable - Annual Real Benefit		
	Households in Any Subsidy Program	Public Housing Households	Households in Other Subsidized Housing Programs
Annual real income in thousands	-35.52 (3.38)	-58.36 (5.74)	8.58 (0.32)
Annual real income squared	.3045 (1.08)	.6138 (2.27)	.1430 (0.19)
Race of head (1 if nonwhite; 0 otherwise)	72.60 (1.34)	-21.53 (0.40)	105.75 (0.81)
Sex of head (1 if female; 0 otherwise)	118.26 (2.11)	84.02 (1.53)	102.80 (0.74)
Age of head in years	8.15 (0.77)	8.77 (0.84)	25.04 (0.98)
Age of head squared	.0493 (0.42)	.0258 (0.23)	-.1353 (0.48)
Education of head in years	8.70 (0.32)	17.01 (0.63)	-.2938 (0.004)
Education squared	-1.79 (1.34)	-2.07 (1.60)	-2.08 (0.60)
Household size	98.48 (2.00)	78.52 (1.66)	86.77 (0.68)
Household size squared	-4.26 (0.80)	-.0701 (0.01)	-16.66 (1.13)
Region of residence: Northeast (1 if NE; 0 otherwise)	-120.88 (1.62)	-190.85 (2.52)	-161.96 (0.96)
Northcentral (1 if NC; 0 otherwise)	-222.97 (3.06)	-331.81 (4.47)	-62.28 (0.38)
South (1 if South; 0 otherwise) (NE=NC=S=0 if West)	-236.55 (3.44)	-414.29 (6.07)	17.94 (0.11)
Place size:			
MEDSMSA (1 if small or medium SMSA; 0 otherwise)	-117.77 (1.58)	-129.97 (1.82)	-132.48 (0.68)
Nonmetro (1 if nonmetropolitan area; 0 otherwise)	-124.83 (1.83)	-116.90 (1.81)	-329.13 (1.78)
Rural (1 if rural area; 0 otherwise)	-58.57 (0.73)	-49.46 (0.65)	-284.41 (1.26)
(MEDSMSA=Nonmetro=Rural=0 if large SMSA)			
Constant	373.68	761.36	-294.85
\bar{R}^2	.18	.30	.07
Standard error	769.57	643.54	951.29
Number of observations	1088	804	284

NOTE: t statistics in parentheses.

TABLE 5.13

TEST FOR NONLINEARITIES

Subsidy Group	F Statistic	Degrees of Freedom
Households in any subsidy program	.9686	(4;1075)
Public housing households	1.966	(4;791)
Households in other sub-sidized housing programs	.4813	(4;271)

real income rises, with benefit reaching a minimum when income is $58,325, *ceteris paribus*. Annual real benefit rises at an increasing rate as age of the head increases. Annual benefit rises at a decreasing rate as household size or education of the head increases, with benefit reaching a maximum when household size equals 11.56 members or when the head has slightly more than a first-grade education, *ceteris paribus*. To test the hypotheses that the coefficients of annual real income squared, age of head squared, education squared, and household size squared are simultaneously equal to zero, F statistics for the three subsidy groups are computed. The test results are presented in Table 5.13. In all cases, the null hypothesis, coefficients equal zero, cannot be rejected.

As noted in Section 4.7, thirty-seven households are omitted from the sample of subsidized households because they have insufficient income to purchase the committed quantities of housing and nonhousing goods over their planning horizons. These households tend to be public housing residents and to have substantially less income, less education, and to be smaller than other public housing households in the sample. They are also more likely to have older, nonwhite, and female heads and to live in the South. The benefit regression for public housing households (column 2, Table 5.10) indicates that most of these characteristics are associated with larger benefits. Specifically, poorer, older, less educated, or female-headed households have larger benefits while smaller households or those located in the South have smaller benefits relative to other public housing residents. Race of head of household is an insignificant determinant of public housing benefit. Overall, the omission of these households is likely to bias mean annual benefit in the downward direction.

5.3 Comparisons with previous work

Previous studies of the benefits of government housing subsidy pro-
grams have focused largely on individual housing programs in a few
selected cities. In addition, those studies that have used a Hicksian
benefit measure have assumed a one-year planning horizon and a one-
year utility function. In this study, the focus is on rental housing sub-
sidy programs taken as a whole across the entire nation, and benefit is
measured assuming an intertemporal utility function and budget con-
straint with a fifty-four-year planning horizon.

Because of the differences in methodology and data between this
and other housing studies, uniformity in results is not to be expected.
Nevertheless, comparison of the results can indicate in a broad sense
how estimates of the magnitude and distribution of benefits differ
when we study the rental housing subsidy system as a whole rather
than selecting individual programs, and when we use an intertemporal
instead of a single-period model. Since I can separate public housing
residents from participants in other subsidy programs, I can also com-
pare my results for the public housing program to results of studies
that have looked either at public housing in different years or in a few
selected cities.

Two common findings of previous housing studies were that, for the
particular program being investigated, tenant benefit tends to be
greater for large households and to vary widely among similar partici-
pating households. The results of this study strongly support the con-
clusion that there is not equal treatment of similar households in the
subsidy programs. Equal treatment is difficult as long as the subsidy
programs provide for construction or substantial rehabilitation of hous-
ing units. This is because housing units deteriorate even with optimal
maintenance and there is no existing mechanism for placing similar
families in units of equal quality. Elimination of this defect within the
present subsidy system would require either increased maintenance of
the older units or variations in rent according to unit quality.

Also, for the public housing programs, as well as for the subsidy
programs taken as a whole, the results strongly indicate that benefit
tends to rise as household size increases. However, when we turn to
subsidy programs other than public housing, the results suggest that
household size is a weak determinant of tenant benefit, and that for
these programs smaller families tend to have larger benefits.

Most of the previous studies have also found a significant, negative
relationship between tenant benefit and household income. For the
subsidy programs as a whole and for public housing, my results support

this conclusion that benefit falls as household income rises. But for other subsidy programs, I find household income to be a positive, but insignificant, determinant of household benefit. This weak relationship between benefit and income for housing programs other than public housing does correspond to results from two previous studies: De-Salvo's (1975) study of New York City's Mitchell–Lama program and the National Housing Policy Review Taskforce's (HUD 1974) study of the Section 236 program.

For the Mitchell–Lama program a negative and insignificant relationship between benefit and household income was found. For the Section 236 program, a positive and insignificant relationship between benefit and income was found. This evidence suggests that, on the one hand, income is an important determinant of benefit to public housing participants and benefit is larger for poorer public housing residents. On the other hand, for participants in other programs, household income does not matter much in determining household benefit.

Five studies have used a Hicksian benefit measure to determine benefit to households participating in the public housing program. Murray (1975) looked at public housing in seven cities in 1968; Olsen and Barton (1983) looked at public housing in New York City in 1965 and 1968; Kraft and Olsen (1977) looked at public housing in five cities in 1972; U.S. Department of Housing and Urban Development (1974) looked at public housing in eleven cities in 1972; and Clemmer (1984) looked at public housing in thirty-three SMSAs in 1977. Mean annual benefit determined by these studies ranges in constant 1977 dollars from $356 (Murray for single-person households) to $1,764 (Clemmer). Mean annual benefit as estimated in this study for public housing nationwide in 1977 is $731, within the range of previous estimates.

Several of these studies (Kraft and Olsen, Olsen and Barton, U.S. Department of Housing and Urban Development) also investigated changes in consumption patterns resulting from one year's participation in public housing. My estimate of the aggregate increase in consumption of housing services by public housing participants is 41 percent, comparable to the previous estimates which range from 33 to 71 percent. However, my estimated aggregate increase in consumption of nonhousing goods is only 1.6 percent – substantially lower than the previous estimates, which are clustered around 14 to 17 percent.

This large difference in my estimates and other estimates of the effect of public housing on nonhousing consumption may be attributable to the intertemporal model. My results suggest that households on average plan to spread over several years the decrease in expenditure on housing that results from one more year's participation in public

housing. Thus, in the current year 1977, the increase in consumption of nonhousing goods is small. Previous studies do not account for the possibility that planned future consumption is affected by one more year's participation in a public housing program. Those studies assume that changes in consumption of both housing and nonhousing goods occur entirely in the current year. This results in larger estimated changes in consumption of nonhousing goods in the year of participation. In my model the effect of the subsidy on consumption of housing in the current year is large relative to the effects on current consumption of nonhousing goods and future consumption of housing. This is to be expected because the in-kind nature of the subsidy constrains changes in housing consumption to occur largely within the year of participation.

CHAPTER 6

Summary and conclusion

6.1 Summary

This study presents empirical evidence on the benefits of federal, state, and local government-subsidized rental housing programs in 1977. Specifically, I estimate:

1. The benefits of the programs to participating families.
2. The changes in consumption of housing and nonhousing goods resulting from participation in the programs.
3. The relationship between mean household benefit and household characteristics.
4. The distribution of benefits among similar families.

Chapter 1 includes an overview of the major federal government rental housing subsidy programs and of New York State's Mitchell–Lama program, an important nonfederal program. The federal programs include low-rent public housing as well as the Section 236 rental housing assistance program, the rent supplement program, the Section 8 new construction and substantial rehabilitation program, and the Section 8 existing housing program. These programs differ according to the subsidy mechanism used and the extent of the subsidy. Their primary goal is to induce low- and moderate-income families to occupy better housing than they would with equally costly cash grants.

The first chapter also includes a summary of the methodological approach used to estimate benefits. The estimates are obtained using a Hicksian measure of consumer surplus within an intertemporal framework. The model assumes an intertemporal utility function and allows future income and prices to affect current consumption decisions. It also allows households to save and dissave. The measure of benefit is the size of the one-year unrestricted cash grant that, if given to the family at the beginning of the current year in place of that year's participation in a housing program, would make the family indifferent

between termination of the housing program at the beginning of the current year and termination at the beginning of the next year.

The data are taken from the national sample of the 1977 Annual Housing Survey. The sample used includes only households living in rental housing. Households located in the New York City SMSA are not included because of the prevalence of rent controls in that city. Households with nonrelative members are also excluded because of the inability to separate the characteristics of the primary family from those of the nonrelatives. The Annual Housing Survey contains extensive information on the characteristics of households and the structural and financial characteristics of the housing units they occupy. In addition, the data identify whether the housing unit is in a public housing project, or is private subsidized housing, or private unsubsidized housing.

Chapter 2 reviews the studies of housing subsidy programs that employ the indifference map approach to measuring tenant benefit according to Hicks' concept of price equivalent variation of income. My model is an extension of the models developed in these studies. Standard practice has been to assume that the preferences of participating households can be represented by a particular one-year utility function that contains housing services and nonhousing goods as its two arguments. It is assumed that households make consumption decisions for the current year without regard to expectations for the future, and that households spend all of their current income in the current year. The benefit measure typically used is the size of the cash grant given to the family in place of participation in a housing program in the current year, which would leave the family as well off without the housing program as with it.

DeSalvo (1971a) was the first to apply this methodology to housing subsidy programs. In a later paper he applied it to New York City's Mitchell–Lama housing program (DeSalvo 1975). He assumes a one-year Cobb–Douglas utility function and derives a benefit expression from this utility function. With this benefit formula, benefit is a function of household income, market rent of the subsidized housing unit, household expenditures on nonhousing goods (measured as the excess of current income over tenant rent), and the household's rent-to-income ratio in the absence of any subsidy. DeSalvo uses expert opinions as estimates of market rent. He estimates the rent-to-income ratio of subsidized households by regressing the ratio of unsubsidized households on their characteristics, and substituting the characteristics of subsidized households into the estimated equation.

Kraft and Olsen (1977) apply the methodology used by DeSalvo to public housing in five cities for 1972, but they use a more sophisticated

method to estimate market rents. Gillingham (1973) had previously estimated relationships between market rent and housing characteristics for the same five cities for 1960. Kraft and Olsen substitute housing characteristics of the public housing units in their sample into Gillingham's hedonic rent equations and adjust with BLS price indices to predict 1972 market rents.

The National Housing Policy Review Taskforce (HUD 1974) applies the methodology, without attempting to improve it, to the housing programs suspended in 1973 by President Nixon. Of the programs evaluated, three are rental housing subsidy programs – public housing, Section 236 rental housing assistance, and the rent supplement program.

Murray (1975) applies the methodology developed by DeSalvo and Kraft and Olsen to a study of public housing in seven cities for 1968. He estimates the parameters of three one-year utility functions – the Cobb–Douglas, the constant elasticity of substitution (CES), and the generalized CES – in order to test whether the true specification is Cobbs–Douglas or ordinary CES. He also uses a hedonic rent equation to predict market rents by adapting to his study an equation relating market rent to housing characteristics that had been estimated by Olsen (1972) for New York City for 1968. Murray's results lead him to uniformly reject the Cobb–Douglas as the correct utility function specification. He also finds that benefit estimates based on the Cobb–Douglas and the generalized CES functions exhibit significantly different distributional patterns, although there is not much difference in estimated means.

In an attempt to use a utility function more general than the Cobb–Douglas, but one that yields a more easily estimated benefit formula than the generalized CES, Olsen and Barton (1983) assume a one-year Stone–Geary utility function in their study of public housing in New York City for 1965 and 1968. To determine market rents they regress rent of private rental housing units on housing characteristics and use the estimated equations to predict market rent for the public housing units. They estimate the parameters of the utility function by stratifying families living in private housing into family types by age, marital status, and race of head of household, and household size. In Olsen and Barton's estimation the parameter that is usually interpreted as subsistence quantity of nonhousing goods is negative for each of twenty household types in each year of their sample. They suggest that the negative signs are due to the fact that their model is a one-year model that does not allow for saving and dissaving.

Because the studies just described concern different programs and use different methods and data, uniformity of results is not to be

expected. Nevertheless, a few common findings emerge. Each of the studies finds that benefits vary widely among similar participating families. In addition, they find mean benefit is positively related to household size and negatively related to household income, although the latter relationship is sometimes insignificant. No consensus emerges with regard to the relationship between mean benefit and age, sex, or race of head of household. Estimated mean annual benefit in the different studies varies from $356 to $855. Estimates of the aggregate increase in housing consumption due to participation in a housing program range from 33 to 71 percent, and estimates of the aggregate increase in the consumption of nonhousing goods are concentrated between 14 and 17 percent.

Chapter 3 begins with a discussion of the theory of intertemporal consumer demand, originally developed by Fisher (1954) and Hicks (1946). In traditional single-period consumer demand theory, consumers are assumed to spend their entire income during the current period and to maximize a utility function that depends only on the commodities consumed during that period. One criticism of this theory is that it requires consumers to be myopic by constraining current consumption decisions to be based solely on present realities, with future expectations playing no role. Intertemporal demand theory drops the assumption of myopia and analyzes the behavior of consumers who plan for the future.

Within the intertemporal framework, a representative consumer is assumed to choose in the current period an optimal consumption plan for every year in his planning horizon, by maximizing his intertemporal utility function subject to his wealth constraint. The traditional budget constraint, requiring that current income equal current expenditures, is inappropriate in an intertemporal framework because it ignores saving or dissaving. A more appropriate budget constraint is one that requires the present values of the income and consumption expenditure streams to be equated over the consumer's planning horizon. With this constraint, saving or dissaving may occur in any one year, but there is no net saving over the entire planning horizon.

In summary, with the intertemporal framework a consumer's chosen consumption plan depends not only on current income and prices but also on future prices, income, and interest rates (which the consumer regards as certain). The consumer makes his current consumption decisions in the current period and, at the same time, plans his future consumption expenditures. This does not necessarily mean that the future consumption plans are carried out. Instead, the consumer is assumed to reconsider his current and future consumption plans every

period, and if his expectations of future prices, income, and interest rates are unchanged, and his tastes are unchanged, his predetermined consumption plan is carried out. Otherwise, the consumer repudiates his past plans and replans his consumption program based on the new information.

Chapter 3 goes on to describe the intertemporal model used to derive a measure of benefit to households participating in subsidized housing programs. The model uses an intertemporal Stone–Geary utility function. The wealth constraint sets discounted, deflated expenditures on housing services and nonhousing goods equal to discounted, deflated income over the household's planning horizon. Each household's planning horizon is assumed equal to the number of years remaining in the expected life of the household head after his entry into the workforce.

Expenditure functions are derived for housing and nonhousing goods for each year of the planning horizon for households who have no plans to participate in a housing subsidy program at any time. These expenditure functions for different types of nonparticipating households are used to estimate the parameters of the utility function. It is assumed that these estimates are applicable to similar type subsidized households. In order to develop the benefit measure and to investigate consumption changes, consumption patterns and utility levels given three alternative states are compared:

1. At the beginning of its planning horizon the household plans to participate in a housing program for a certain number of years that include the current year but no future years.
2. The household learns at the beginning of the current year that the program will be immediately and permanently terminated.
3. The household learns that it will be given a cash grant in the current year in place of its planned participation in a housing program in that year.

Demand equations are estimated for housing and nonhousing goods for each year in the household's planning horizon for these three alternative states, under the assumption that household expectations of prices, income, participation in a housing program, and interest rates relevant at the beginning of the household's planning horizon have been realized up to the beginning of the current year. The benefit measure is derived from these demand equations and from the household utility function. This measure is interpreted as the size of the one-year cash grant, which enables the household to reach a level of utility without participation in a housing subsidy program in the cur-

rent year or beyond that is identical to the utility level reached given participation in the current year but no future years.

In order to implement the model developed in Chapter 3, it is necessary to estimate several variables ranging from the real rate of interest to household lifetime income. Acceptance of the final results must be tempered by the fact that they are based on the many assumptions made in estimating these variables. Nevertheless, the results may provide reasonable indications of the order of magnitude of the effects of the subsidies. More importantly, they illustrate how an intertemporal model can be used to estimate the effects of subsidy programs.

Chapter 4 describes the procedures used to estimate the necessary variables. The model assumes a household planning horizon at entry into the labor force equal to the remainder of the household head's life expectancy. This planning horizon is set at fifty-four years for each household based on an assumed common entry age of twenty-one and death at seventy-five. The model allows different households to have participated in a housing subsidy program for different lengths of time. Length of past participation is estimated with data from the AHS on the year the head of household moved into his present housing unit.

An estimate of the real interest rate is needed to discount future planned payments and receipts. According to Fisherian interest theory, nominal interest rates differ from real rates because of expected future rates of inflation. Several studies have examined the effect of inflationary expectations on the nominal interest rates on U.S. Treasury securities. In these studies the practical problem is to find a measure of inflationary expectations. Tanzi (1980) estimates the relationship between nominal interest rates and inflationary expectations with interest data from 1952 to 1975 on twelve-month Treasury securities. He uses six alternative measures of inflationary expectations and controls for cyclical fluctuations in economic activity. His estimates of the real interest rate on twelve-month bills average 3.20, with 2.91 the estimate from the best-fitting equation. In light of Tanzi's evidence, which is in line with estimates from previous studies, 3.00 is used as an estimate of the real rate of interest.

The model assumes that prices of housing and nonhousing goods change at the same rate over time. This assumption allows use of current prices as estimates of both past and expected future relative prices. The Bureau of Labor Statistics' (1979) intermediate budget for a four-person household is used to obtain a price index for nonhousing goods. The BLS data are reported for forty large and small SMSAs and for four regional nonmetropolitan areas. A housing price index is obtained by supplementing the BLS data with the Urban Institute's

(Follain et al. 1979) place-to-place, constant quality indices of housing prices. The latter are calculated for thirty-nine large SMSAs.

Other authors have been criticized for using the BLS budget data to construct price indices. The data have two shortcomings. First, the quality of the BLS standard market basket is not constant across cities. Second, the market basket was priced in 1967 and has been updated since then with components of the CPI. These revisions may not accurately adjust the prices for changes over time. The Urban Institute's housing price index is based on more recent data (1974 and 1975) than the BLS index and has more extensive controls for housing quality. Consequently, Urban Institute housing prices are used in place of the BLS housing prices when the former are available.

The model assumes that households equate their consumption expenditures and income receipts, not necessarily in any one year, but over the entire planning horizon. It also assumes that household decisions regarding expenditures are based on current income and expectations of future income. Therefore it is necessary to have an estimate of each household's stream of income over its fifty-four-year planning horizon. Using the 1977 AHS data, current household income is regressed on a set of household characteristics that are presumed to determine income for four household types. The households are distinguished by their race and their participation in a housing subsidy program. The estimated equations are used to determine expected income for each household in every year in its planning horizon. These annual estimates of income are combined with estimates of the exogenous growth rate of real income to generate an expected income stream for each household over its planning horizon.

In choosing the household characteristics expected to determine household income, I use human capital theory. This theory contends that an individual's real earnings are related to past investments in human capital. I also assume that demographic variables affect income.

The logarithm of annual household income from all sources in 1977 is the dependent variable in the income-generating functions. The broad classes of independent variables include education of head, experience of head (measured by his age and current employment status), sex and marital status of head, size and age composition of the household, sources of household income, and location of the household. To estimate income for each year, these variables with the exception of age of head (which varies from twenty-one to seventy-four) are held constant at their 1977 levels. The income estimates are adjusted by the geometric average rate of change in output per person-hour in the nonfarm business sector of the economy from 1948 to 1978.

In order to estimate benefit I also need estimates of the subsidized and market rents of the subsidized housing units during the years of each household's participation. The subsidized rent for 1977 is contained in the data. Subsidized rents for previous years of participation are estimated by assuming that the ratio of subsidized rent to income is constant over the entire period. This rent-to-income ratio is computed by dividing the 1977 subsidized rent by predicted income for 1977 for each household and multiplying this estimated ratio by predicted income for previous years of participation. This provides estimates of subsidized rents in the previous years.

Hedonic pricing techniques are used to estimate market rents. Monthly gross rent of unsubsidized housing units is regressed on a set of thirty-three housing characteristics. Separate market rent equations are estimated for whites and nonwhites to allow for the possibility that they face different housing prices. The regression coefficients and the characteristics of subsidized units are used to estimate their market rent.

Initially, I use market rent as the dependent variable. It has been suggested that number of rooms might be a source of heteroskedasticity in the market rent equations. Using the F test suggested by Goldfeld and Quandt (1965), the null hypothesis of homoskedasticity is rejected for both the white and nonwhite equations. To reduce the problem of heteroskedasticity each variable is divided by number of rooms. The estimated weighted least-squares regressions are used to estimate monthly gross rent per room of each subsidized housing unit. Annual market rent is calculated by multiplying predicted monthly rent per room by twelve and multiplying the resulting product by the number of rooms in the unit.

Nonlinear least-squares estimation of the housing expenditure equations of nonparticipating households yields consistent estimates of the utility function parameters. These parameters are estimated using the 1977 data for the sample of nonparticipating households, stratified into sixteen types by race, region, and household size. In order to help ensure that the household's utility function is defined, the parameter B_h is constrained to be less than the minimum value of the quantity of housing services consumed by participating households of a particular type. The constrained estimates of the utility function parameters are applied to participating families of the same type when household benefit is estimated.

Chapter 5 contains the empirical results. To facilitate comparison of the results with results of previous studies of the same type, most of which analyze public housing, the results are reported separately for

the housing subsidy programs combined, the public housing program, and other housing subsidy programs.

The results indicate that, in aggregate, subsidized households consumed around 40 percent more housing and 1.7 percent more nonhousing goods in 1977 than they would have consumed in the absence of the programs in that year. However, 11 percent of all subsidized households, 9 percent of public housing households, and 17 percent of households in other subsidy programs occupied worse housing as a result of participation in the programs. The estimate of mean annual benefit from participation in a housing subsidy program in 1977 is $633. Mean annual benefit for the public housing program is $731 and for other housing subsidy programs only $379.

The housing programs reduce the effective market price of housing to subsidized families by a substantial amount: 42 percent on average for all subsidized households, 45 percent for public housing households, and 33 percent for participants in other housing programs. There is also a substantial difference, approximately $413, between mean annual benefit and mean annual subsidy (computed as the difference between subsidized rent and predicted market rent). Replacing the housing programs with unrestricted cash grants of the same amount, distributed in 1977 only, would increase aggregate benefit to participants in all programs by 66 percent on average (55 percent for public housing households; 114 percent for households receiving other housing subsidies).

These in-kind housing programs are not valued solely by participating households. Presumably, they are also valued by taxpayers especially if they induce participating households to consume more housing and less nonhousing goods than they would if given cash grants that allow them to buy a combination of goods with the same market value as the combination consumed under the programs. The results show that the subsidy programs have the desired effects on both housing and nonhousing expenditures. In the aggregate, one-year cash grants equal to the housing subsidies would decrease housing consumption by around 28 percent relative to consumption with the subsidy programs. In addition, relative to the subsidy programs, cash grants would increase consumption of nonhousing goods by approximately 1.8 percent.

The programs' effects on future planned consumption are also investigated. The results show that the expectation of being able to participate in a subsidized housing program in 1977 leads to a slight increase in planned consumption of housing in future years, even though the programs are assumed to be unavailable after 1977. If the in-kind subsidy programs were replaced with one-year cash grants, households

would plan to consume yet a bit more housing in each of the future years. Thus, although the subsidized housing programs are more stimulative of housing consumption than cash grants in 1977, they are slightly less stimulative of housing consumption in future years. In addition, the subsidized housing programs and cash grants have larger effects on planned future consumption of nonhousing goods than on planned future consumption of housing, although cash grants are more stimulative of nonhousing consumption in all years than the in-kind subsidy programs.

Finally, the distribution of the benefits of the subsidy programs is investigated. Subsidized households on average are quite different from the average U.S. household. Subsidized households are likely to be poorer, more likely to live in the South or West, and have younger, nonwhite, and female heads than the average U.S. household. Cross tabulations of benefits by income class that control for household size suggest that benefit decreases as income of participating families rises, but that the variance in benefit among families in the same income class is substantial.

To further investigate the distributive effects of the programs, annual real benefit is regressed on household characteristics for the subsidy programs combined, the public housing program, and the other subsidy programs. All of the regressions have small coefficients of determination and large standard errors, indicating enormous variation in real benefit among similar households. The results for the combined programs and the public housing program also indicate clearly that, on average, real benefit is greater for poorer and larger households and those with older, female, or less educated heads. Real benefit is smaller for households living in the Northcentral or South or in small or medium SMSAs and nonmetropolitan areas. Race of head is an insignificant determinant of real benefit. For the sample of households in other subsidized housing programs, the results are quite different. Except for age and education of head, and location in a nonmetropolitan area, all the household characteristics are insignificant explanatory variables.

Comparing these estimates of average benefit and increases in housing consumption to results of previous studies, I find that my estimates are within the range of the previous estimates. However, my estimates for increases in consumption of nonhousing goods are substantially lower (a less than 2 percent increase compared to 14 to 17 percent increase). This large difference may be explained by the intertemporal model. With the intertemporal model, households are allowed to spread over many years the increase in consumption of nonhousing

goods that results from one more year's participation in an in-kind subsidy program. With the one-year model used in other studies, any change in consumption is constrained to occur in the current year only.

Comparing welfare distributional effects, the results strongly support the consensus of previous studies that benefits vary widely among similar subsidized households. Two other conclusions frequently drawn from empirical studies are that benefit and household size are positively correlated and that benefit is negatively correlated with household income. For the subsidy programs as a whole and for public housing, the results strongly support these conclusions. For other subsidy programs, however, I find positive but weak relationships between benefit and both household size and income.

6.2 Conclusion

The system of rental housing subsidy programs that has been analyzed was designed primarily to induce low- and moderate-income families to occupy better housing than they would without the subsidies. The results confirm that the present system of in-kind subsidies does increase housing consumption of participating families. I find that, in the aggregate, subsidized families consumed 40 percent more housing in 1977 than they would have in the absence of the programs. In addition, I find that consumption of nonhousing goods also increased as a result of the housing subsidies, but by less than 2 percent in 1977. I estimate that the value participating families attach to these changes in consumption patterns is significant although the estimates of benefit are not as large as most previous estimates. I find that, on average, subsidized families would require $633 in cash to induce them to move out of their subsidized units. Public housing residents place a higher value on their participation, $731, while residents of other programs value their participation by a substantially lower amount, $379. These benefits are equivalent to a 6 to 10 percent increase in income.

However, I also find that there is a substantial difference (over $400) between the mean annual benefit and the mean annual subsidy provided by the programs. This difference stems from the subsidies' in-kind nature. Thus, if we are concerned solely with helping low-income families and if we consider them to be the best judges of what is best for themselves, we should replace the in-kind subsidies with unrestricted cash grants. We could increase the perceived benefit to subsidized families by 66 percent at the same taxpayer cost. Or, we could decrease taxpayer cost by 39 percent while maintaining the per-

ceived welfare of participating families at the levels resulting from participation in the in-kind subsidy programs.

The goal of the housing programs, however, is not just to increase the welfare of the subsidized families but also to increase their consumption of housing beyond what would result from unrestricted cash grants. I find that while a cash grant program does tend to increase consumption of both housing and nonhousing goods relative to consumption in the absence of any subsidy, cash grants are less stimulative of housing consumption and more stimulative of nonhousing consumption than these programs. Thus, the results support the conclusions of previous studies. One interesting result of this study, though, is that when we look at the effects of cash grants and in-kind subsidies in future years, we find that while the in-kind programs are more stimulative of housing consumption in the current year, cash grants are more stimulative of housing consumption in future years.

Evaluating how well the programs work also depends on determining who is served. The goals of the programs are to help low- and moderate-income families. In addition, the programs are often designed to favor families with elderly or handicapped heads, families with a veteran or member of the armed forces, and families displaced by urban renewal.

I find that the average subsidized household is, in fact, poorer than the average U.S. household and that for all participating families, benefit falls as income rises. However, for participants in subsidy programs other than public housing benefit rises as income rises. This latter result suggests that programs other than public housing are not well-focused redistributive devices. With regard to age of head, I find that for all participating families benefit rises with age.

Furthermore, the results lead me to conclude that there is not equal treatment of similar families in the subsidy programs. Equal treatment is not to be expected as long as the subsidy programs provide for construction or substantial rehabilitation of housing units. This is because there is no existing mechanism for placing similar families in units of equal quality. Elimination of this defect within the present subsidy system would require either increased maintenance of the older units or variations in rent according to unit quality.

An alternative to the present system of subsidy programs is a housing allowance program. With housing allowances, we could combine some of the good qualities of an unrestricted cash grant program with those of the in-kind subsidy programs. With a housing allowance program, families would be given a cash grant on the condition that they occupy housing that meets certain standards. By varying the size of

grant according to household income and size, we could accomplish the goal of providing "decent" housing to low-income families. At the same time we could reduce the inequities of the current programs by offering the same grant to similar households and by discontinuing construction of new subsidized housing.

Prices of nonhousing goods and housing services by SMSA and region (1976)

PRICES OF NONHOUSING GOODS AND HOUSING SERVICES BY SMSA AND REGION (1976)

AHS-Identified SMSA	SMSA Identified in Price Source	Price of Nonhousing Goods (P_x)	Price of Housing Services (P_h)
Northeast			
Albany-Schenectady-Troy, NY	UI	$10,953	$2,455
Allentown-Bethlehem, PA-NY		10,953	1,916
Binghamton, NY-PA		10,953	1,916
Boston, MA	UI & BLS	12,222	2,403
Bridgeport, CT		10,953	1,916
Buffalo, NY	BLS	10,834	2,058
Erie, PA		10,953	1,916
Harrisburg, PA		10,953	1,916
Hartford, CT	UI & BLS	11,470	2,477
Jersey City, NJ		10,953	1,916
Johnstown, PA		10,953	1,916
Lancaster, PA	BLS	10,006	1,917
New Haven, CT		10,953	1,916
New York, NY[a]		---	---
Newark, NJ	UI	10,953	3,055
Paterson-Clifton-Passaic, NJ	UI	10,953	2,821
Philadelphia, PA	UI & BLS	10,882	1,718
Pittsburgh, PA	UI & BLS	10,172	2,284
Providence-Pawtucket-Warwick, RI-MA		10,953	1,916
Reading, PA		10,953	1,916
Rochester, NY	UI	10,953	1,788
Springfield-Chicopee-Holyoke, MA-CT	UI	10,953	1,955
Syracuse, NY		10,953	1,916
Trenton, NJ		10,953	1,916
Utica-Rome, NY		10,953	1,916
Wilkes-Barre-Hazelton, PA		10,953	1,916
Worcester, MA		10,953	1,916

110

AHS-Identified SMSA	SMSA Identified in Price Source	Price of Nonhousing Goods (P_x)	Price of Housing Services (P_h)
York, PA		10,953	1,916
BLS Weighted Average SMSA Price		10,953	1,915
UI Weighted, Adjusted Average SMSA Price		---	1,916
BLS Nonmetropolitan Area Price		10,460	1,766
North Central			
Akron, OH		10,496	1,779
Appleton-Oshkosh, WI		10,496	1,779
Canton, OH		10,496	1,779
Chicago, IL	UI & BLS	10,667	1,847
Cincinnati, OH-KY-IN	UI & BLS	10,542	1,334
Cleveland, OH	BLS	11,060	1,670
Columbus, OH	UI	10,496	1,366
Davenport-Rock Island-Moline, IA-IL		10,496	1,779
Dayton, OH	BLS	10,121	1,566
Des Moines, IA		10,496	1,779
Detroit, MI	UI & BLS	10,751	1,793
Duluth-Superior, MN-WI		10,496	1,779
Flint, MI		10,496	1,779
Fort Wayne, IN		10,496	1,779
Gary-Hammond-East Chicago, IN		10,496	1,779
Grand Rapids, MI		10,496	1,779
Indianapolis, IN	BLS	10,510	1,791
Kansas City, MO-KS	UI & BLS	10,317	1,149
Lansing, MI		10,496	1,779
Lorain-Elyria, OH		10,496	1,779
Madison, WI	UI	10,496	1,855
Milwaukee, WI	UI & BLS	10,665	1,902
Minneapolis-St. Paul, MN	UI & BLS	10,176	2,397

111

AHS-Identified SMSA	SMSA Identified in Price Source	Price of Nonhousing Goods (P_x)	Price of Housing Services (P_h)
Omaha, NE-IA		10,496	1,779
Peoria, IL		10,496	1,779
Rockford, IL		10,496	1,779
St. Louis, MO-IL	BLS	10,458	1,547
South Bend, IN		10,496	1,779
Toledo, OH-MI		10,496	1,779
Wichita, KS	UI & BLS	9,769	1,355
Youngstown-Warren, OH	UI & BLS	10,496	1,779
BLS SMSA Weighted Average		10,496	1,916
UI SMSA Weighted, Adjusted Average		---	1,779
BLS Nonmetropolitan Area Average		9,526	1,840
South			
Atlanta, GA	UI & BLS	9,958	1,688
Augusta, GA-SC		9,948	1,839
Austin, TX	BLS	9,973	1,506
Baltimore, MD	BLS	9,821	2,141
Baton Rouge, LA	BLS	10,003	1,364
Beaumont-Port Arthur-Orange, TX		9,948	1,839
Birmingham, AL		9,948	1,839
Charleston, SC		9,948	1,839
Charlotte, NC		9,948	1,839
Chattanooga, TN-GA		9,948	1,839
Columbia, SC		9,948	1,839
Corpus Christi, TX		9,948	1,839
Dallas, TX	UI & BLS	9,959	1,697
El Paso, TX		9,948	1,839
Fort Lauderdale-Hollywood, FL		9,948	1,839
Fort Worth, TX	UI	9,948	1,322

112

AHS-Identified SMSA	SMSA Identified in Price Source	Price of Nonhousing Goods (P_x)	Price of Housing Services (P_h)
Greensboro-Winston-Salem, High Point, NC		9,948	1,839
Greenville, SC		9,948	1,839
Houston, TX	BLS	10,184	1,652
Huntington-Ashland, WV-KY-OH		9,948	1,839
Jackson, MS		9,948	1,839
Jacksonville, FL		9,948	1,839
Knoxville, TN		9,948	1,839
Little Rock-North Little Rock, AR		9,948	1,839
Louisville, KY-IN		9,948	1,839
Memphis, TN-AR	UI	9,948	1,699
Miami, FL	UI	9,948	1,699
Mobile, AL		9,948	1,839
Nashville-Davidson, TN	BLS	10,147	1,584
New Orleans, LA	UI	9,948	1,544
Newport News-Hampton, VA		9,948	1,877
Norfolk-Portsmouth, VA		9,948	1,839
Oklahoma City, OK		9,948	1,839
Orlando, FL	UI & BLS	9,577	2,655
Richmond, VA		9,948	1,839
San Antonio, TX	UI	9,948	888
Shreveport, LA		9,948	1,839
Tampa-St. Petersburg, FL		9,948	1,839
Tulsa, OK		9,948	1,839
Washington, DC-MD-VA	UI & BLS	10,499	2,436
West Palm Beach, FL		9,948	1,839
Wilmington, DE-MD-NJ		9,948	1,839
BLS SMSA Weighted Average		9,948	1,759

113

AHS-Identified SMSA	SMSA Identified in Price Source	Price of Nonhousing Goods (P_x)	Price of Housing Services (P_h)
UI SMSA Weighted, Adjusted Average		---	1,839
BLS Nonmetropolitan Area Average		9,459	1,335
West			
Albuquerque, NM		10,302	2,136
Anaheim-Santa Anna-Garden Grove, CA	UI	10,302	3,332
Bakersfield, CA	BLS	9,723	1,824
Denver, CO	BLS	10,527	1,554
Fresno, CA		10,302	2,136
Honolulu, HI	BLS	11,608	2,767
Las Vegas, NV		10,302	2,136
Los Angeles-Long Beach, CA	UI & BLS	10,215	2,039
Oxnard-Ventura, CA		10,302	2,136
Phoenix, AZ	UI	10,302	1,944
Portland, OR-WA	UI	10,302	1,600
Sacramento, CA		10,302	2,136
Salinas-Monterey, CA		10,302	2,136
Salt Lake City, UT	UI	10,302	1,777
San Bernardino-Riverside-Ontario, CA	UI	10,302	1,911
San Diego, CA	UI & BLS	10,380	1,901
San Francisco-Oakland, CA	UI & BLS	10,433	2,275
San Jose, CA		10,302	2,136
Santa Barbara, CA		10,302	2,136
Seattle-Everett, WA	BLS	10,528	2,261
Spokane, WA	UI	10,302	2,122
Stockton, CA		10,302	2,136
Tacoma, WA	UI	10,302	1,933
Tucson, AZ		10,302	2,136

TABLE A.1—Continued

AHS-Identified SMSA	SMSA Identified in Price Source	Price of Nonhousing Goods (P_x)	Price of Housing Services (P_h)
BLS SMSA Weighted Average		10,302	2,097
UI SMSA Weighted, Adjusted Average		---	2,136
BLS Nonmetropolitan Area Average		9,493	1,656
BLS Urban Average (1976)		10,469	1,901

SOURCES: BLS prices are calculated from U.S. Department of Labor (1979, Table 136, p. 487). Urban Institute prices are calculated from Follain, Ozanne and Alburger (1979, Table 20, p. 71).

[a]Households in the New York, New York SMSA were dropped from the sample (see Section 1.3).

Distributions of benefits by income class for public housing residents and residents in other subsidy programs

TABLE B.1

TABLE B.1

DISTRIBUTION OF BENEFITS BY INCOME CLASS FOR ONE- TO TWO-PERSON HOUSEHOLDS IN
LOW-RENT PUBLIC HOUSING (Sample Sizes in Parentheses)

Benefit Class	<$4,000	Income Class $4,000-7,999	$8,000-11,999	≥$12,000	Population Percentage (Sample Size)
<$200	9% (16)	22% (22)	29% (11)	71% (24)	21% (73)
$200-599	5% (9)	18% (18)	34% (13)	18% (6)	13% (46)
$600-999	21% (37)	23% (23)	26% (10)	3% (1)	20% (71)
$1,000-1,399	39% (71)	26% (26)	5% (2)	6% (2)	29% (101)
≥$1,400	26% (47)	11% (11)	5% (2)	3% (1)	17% (61)
Population Percentage (Sample Size)	51% (180)	28% (100)	11% (38)	10% (34)	100% (352)

TABLE B.2

DISTRIBUTION OF BENEFITS BY INCOME CLASS FOR THREE- TO FOUR-PERSON HOUSEHOLDS IN
LOW-RENT PUBLIC HOUSING (Sample Sizes in Parentheses)

Benefit Class	<$4,000	Income Class $4,000-7,999	$8,000-11,999	≥$12,000	Population Percentage (Sample Size)
<$200	14% (13)	22% (16)	26% (30)	54% (31)	31% (90)
$200-599	13% (12)	21% (15)	20% (13)	32% (18)	20% (58)
$600-999	22% (20)	29% (21)	12% (8)	9% (5)	19% (54)
$1,000-1,399	25% (23)	14% (10)	11% (7)	5% (3)	15% (43)
≥$1,400	26% (24)	15% (11)	11% (7)	0% (0)	15% (42)
Population Percentage (Sample Size)	32% (92)	25% (73)	23% (65)	20% (57)	100% (287)

117

TABLE B.3

DISTRIBUTION OF BENEFITS BY INCOME CLASS FOR FIVE OR MORE PERSON HOUSEHOLDS
IN LOW-RENT PUBLIC HOUSING (Sample Sizes in Parentheses)

Benefit Class	Income Class <$4,000	$4,000-7,999	$8,000-11,999	>$12,000	Population Percentage (Sample Size)
<$200	14% (6)	6% (4)	22% (7)	25% (6)	14% (23)
$200-599	10% (4)	13% (9)	28% (9)	25% (6)	17% (28)
$600-999	29% (12)	16% (11)	19% (6)	21% (5)	21% (34)
$1,000-1,399	33% (14)	28% (19)	19% (6)	21% (5)	27% (44)
>$1,400	14% (6)	36% (24)	13% (4)	8% (2)	22% (36)
Population Percentage (Sample Size)	26% (42)	41% (67)	19% (32)	15% (24)	100% (165)

TABLE B.4

DISTRIBUTION OF BENEFITS BY INCOME CLASS FOR ONE- TO TWO-PERSON HOUSEHOLDS IN OTHER
SUBSIDIZED HOUSING PROGRAMS (Sample Sizes in Parentheses)

Benefit Class	Income Class <$4,000	$4,000-7,999	$8,000-11,999	>$12,000	Population Percentage (Sample Size)
<$200	30% (28)	46% (18)	38% (6)	50% (4)	35% (56)
$200-599	10% (9)	10% (4)	44% (7)	38% (3)	15% (23)
$600-999	23% (22)	23% (9)	13% (2)	0% (0)	21% (33)
$1,000-1,399	26% (25)	15% (6)	6% (1)	0% (0)	20% (32)
>$1,400	12% (11)	5% (2)	0% (0)	13% (1)	9% (14)
Population Percentage (Sample Size)	60% (95)	25% (39)	10% (16)	5% (8)	100% (158)

118

DISTRIBUTION OF BENEFITS BY INCOME CLASS FOR THREE- TO FOUR-PERSON HOUSEHOLDS IN OTHER
SUBSIDIZED HOUSING PROGRAMS (Sample Sizes in Parentheses)

| Benefit Class | Income Class | | | | Population Percentage (Sample Size) |
	<$4,000	$4,000-7,999	$8,000-11,999	≥$12,000	
<$200	59% (13)	43% (13)	45% (9)	67% (12)	52% (47)
$200-599	9% (2)	7% (2)	35% (7)	17% (3)	16% (14)
$600-999	5% (1)	13% (4)	15% (3)	6% (1)	10% (9)
$1,000-1,399	9% (2)	10% (3)	5% (1)	6% (1)	8% (7)
≥$1,400	18% (4)	27% (8)	0% (0)	6% (1)	14% (13)
Population Percentage (Sample Size)	24% (22)	33% (30)	22% (20)	20% (18)	100% (90)

TABLE B.6

DISTRIBUTION OF BENEFITS BY INCOME CLASS FOR FIVE OR MORE PERSON HOUSEHOLDS IN
OTHER SUBSIDIZED HOUSING PROGRAMS (Sample Sizes in Parentheses)

| Benefit Class | Income Class | | | | Population Percentage (Sample Size) |
	<$4,000	$4,000-7,999	$8,000-11,999	≥$12,000	
<$200	56% (5)	36% (4)	50% (4)	50% (4)	42% (17)
$200-599	33% (3)	9% (1)	25% (2)	13% (1)	19% (7)
$600-999	11% (1)	27% (3)	13% (1)	13% (1)	17% (6)
$1,000-1,399	0% (0)	9% (1)	13% (1)	13% (1)	8% (3)
≥$1,400	0% (9)	18% (2)	0% (0)	13% (1)	8% (3)
Population Percentage (Sample Size)	25% (9)	31% (11)	22% (8)	22% (8)	100% (36)

119

Notes

Chapter 1

1. This is the stated national housing policy goal of the U.S. Housing Act of 1949.
2. The Section 235 program provides mortgage subsidies to lower-income families for the purchase of new or substantially rehabilitated houses. Participating families buy houses at reduced rates of interest on the mortgage with HUD making up the difference between the family's payment and the amount due the mortgagee based on the market rate of interest.
3. For an in-depth description of federal housing programs and their development, see U.S. Department of Housing and Urban Development (1974) and Weicher (1980).
4. This discussion is based upon U.S. Department of Housing and Urban Development (1974, ch. 4); Weicher (1980, chs. 3 and 4); and U.S. Congress (1977) and (1978).
5. Housing and Urban Development Act of 1965, Section 103(a).
6. Housing and Urban Development Act of 1969, Section 213(a).
7. For a complete description of the 1977 national sample of the Annual Housing Survey, see U.S. Department of Commerce (1979a and b) and U.S. Department of Housing and Urban Development (1979b).
8. One potential problem with the AHS data is that, when compared with HUD data on the actual number of federally subsidized dwellings, the number of AHS households assigning themselves to public housing is too high, whereas the number assigning themselves to other subsidized housing programs is too low. In 1977, according to AHS data, there were 1,897,000 public housing households and 670,000 households in the other subsidy programs. For the same year, HUD reports 1,174,000 public housing units and 1,176,403 other subsidized units (U.S. Department of Commerce, 1979a, part C, p. 5). This raises the possibility of bias in the results. However, the discrepancies may be the result of factors other than reporting errors. For example, part of the discrepancies are due to differences in timing of the AHS and HUD surveys and to the existence of state and local rental housing projects unreported in the HUD data. Adjusting the data to account for the possibility of any remaining report-

120

ing errors would involve a substantial amount of work and is beyond the scope of this study.

Chapter 2

1. For elaboration of this point see Olsen and York (1984, pp. 179–80). Their study also provides empirical evidence for public housing and rent control in New York City in 1965 that suggests that using either the simple subsidy measure or Marshall's consumer surplus measure leads to significantly distorted evidence regarding the distributive effects of these programs.
2. Clemmer (1984) has recently developed an alternative method for measuring equivalent variation based on linear compensated demand functions instead of explicit utility functions.
3. See U.S. Department of Housing and Urban Development (1974).
4. Consumption changes are not estimated for the rent supplement program.
5. Evidence found in Olsen and York (1984, pp. 191–2) supports the notion that distribution of benefits among participating families is affected by choice of utility function. Like Murray they conclude that the Cobb–Douglas specification should be avoided in favor of more general utility functions.

Chapter 3

1. Hicks (1946, p. 122) calls these discrete periods "weeks."
2. Yaari (1964b) and Arrow and Kurz (1969) investigate the implications of extending the consumer's planning horizon to infinity.
3. Fisher (1954, p. 61). Fisher analyzes the forces that may cause the degree of impatience to vary from individual to individual and over time. According to Fisher, impatience may vary with the characteristics of individuals, and the size, time shape, and probability of expected income streams. For example, the greater an expected increase in future income, the more impatient the consumer will be for present over future goods.
4. Hu (1980) and Wu (1974) explore the implications for the consumer's lifetime allocation process of imperfect capital markets where certain limitations on borrowing exist. Arrow and Kurz (1969) restrict borrowing even further. They assume that consumer nonhuman capital must always be positive, which implies that there can be no borrowing out of future labor income.
5. This idea forms the basis for the permanent income and life-cycle theories of consumption. See Friedman (1957) and Modigliani and Brumberg (1954).
6. It is straightforward to relax these assumptions and consider a budget constraint that allows initial and terminal bondholdings to be different from zero. See, for example, Yaari (1964a) and Dixon et al. (1980).
7. See Hu (1980), Diewert (1974), and Dixon et al. (1980) for an analysis of

intertemporal behavior when the consumer can accumulate stocks of durable goods.

8. The spot price p_{jt} is the amount that must be paid in period t for delivery of one unit of good j in period t (see Pollak 1975, p. 181).

9. Taking the length of the discrete period to be one year can be justified on grounds that variation in relative prices of the two composite goods within a year is likely to be small (Diewert 1974, p. 507).

10. This assumption is consistent with the finding of Muth (1960) and Smith (1976). DeLeeuw and Ekanem (1971) present conflicting evidence implying that price elasticity of the long-run supply of housing services is between 0.3 and 0.7. Reanalysis of their model by Grieson (1973) and Vaughn (1976) suggests a much higher elasticity.

11. We are interested in the consumption program for non-participating households because only these households have a continuous budget frontier. Estimation of the parameters of the utility function based on data for households facing discontinuous budget frontiers is considerably more difficult (see Hausman and Wise 1980). The expenditure functions for nonparticipants are used to estimate the parameters of the utility functions for subsidized households with similar characteristics (see Section 4.7). The nonparticipants' expenditure curves are derived for every year of their planning horizons. The issue of selection bias is addressed in Section 4.7.

12. Deaton and Muellbauer (1980, p. 122) suggest that this is the most useful assumption to make regarding consumer expectations about changes in relative prices in future periods.

13. This system of expenditure equations derived for single-period consumption analysis is known as the linear expenditure system. It satisfies all the general restrictions implied by the axioms of the theory of consumer choice, including homogeneity, adding up, negativity of the direct substitution effect, and symmetry of cross-substitution effects provided that $0 < \gamma_i < 1$, $H_{it} - B_h > 0$, and $X_{it} - B_x > 0$ (see Phlips 1974, pp. 121–7).

14. The Stone–Geary utility function was originally developed by Klein and Rubin (1947–48), Samuelson (1947–48), Geary (1950–51), and Stone (1954). See Phlips (1974, pp. 121–6) for a history of its development.

15. See Phlips (1974, pp. 127–31) for an overview of studies applying the linear expenditure system. Olsen and Barton (1983) derive the benefit formula for a one-period Stone–Geary utility function in order to calculate the benefits of public housing.

16. DeSalvo (1975), Murray (1975), and Kraft and Olsen (1977) use the Cobb–Douglas specification to calculate benefits of housing programs. The Cobb–Douglas utility function is a restricted form of the Stone–Geary utility function, where $B_h = B_x = 0$.

17. Murray (1975, p. 774) uses an iterative computer program to approximate benefits of public housing using a generalized constant elasticity of substitution utility function.

18. Mayo also suggests that future research might explore the translog utility

function or the quadratic expenditure system, which are less restrictive than the Stone–Geary utility function with respect to income and price elasticities.

19. I assume that news of the termination of the housing programs is the only change in the household's circumstances or expectations. I assume that the members of the household choose the same job and work the same number of hours as before and that there is no change in the tax payments of the family or in the quantities of other public services received by the family.

20. Note that to a first approximation most rental housing subsidy programs offer eligible families specific dwelling units. The programs do not simply rotate budget constraints.

21. Note that consumption in future periods is also affected.

Chapter 4

1. Diewert (1974) makes a similar assumption in his attempt to estimate a model of intertemporal consumption behavior. He assumes a common planning horizon of thirty years across all households.

2. The median age bracket of household heads in the sample is 30 to 34. For this age group in 1976, life expectancy was 75.3 years (see U.S. Department of Health, Education, and Welfare 1978, Table 5.1).

3. Because of the assumption that all heads of households enter the workforce at twenty-one, k_i is constrained to be equal to or greater than one.

4. In the sample of 1,127 households residing in subsidized rental housing, 94 moved in between 1965 and 1970, 26 between 1960 and 1964, 10 between 1950 and 1959, and 3 before 1950.

5. The BLS prices are taken from U.S. Department of Labor (1979, Table 136, p. 487). I choose the intermediate budget because the sample of households in private rental housing includes a wide distribution of income levels. The Urban Institute prices are taken from Follain et al. (1979, Table 20, p. 71).

6. See, for example, Carliner (1973), Maisel et al. (1971), and DeLeeuw (1971). Mayo (1981, p. 12) gives a concise overview of the variety of measures of relative housing prices that have been used in various analyses. Polinsky and Ellwood (1979) criticize price variables used in previous housing demand studies.

7. See Follain et al. (1979, Table 19, p. 70) for a description of the housing characteristics used in the hedonic regressions.

8. The 125 SMSAs identified by the AHS are listed in Appendix A, U.S. Department of Housing and Urban Development (1979a, pp. 56–8). Non-metropolitan areas are places with populations of less than 50,000. Rural areas are places with populations of less than 2,500.

9. See U.S. Department of Labor (1967, Table C-1, p. 89).

10. U.S. Department of Labor (various issues, 1975 and 1976, Table 7).

11. See Mayo (1976, pp. 54–65) for a more complete discussion of these methods.
12. See Champernowne (1978), Brown (1976), Lydall (1976), and Mincer (1976) for a more detailed discussion of stochastic earnings theory.
13. Struyk (1976) also stratifies by race.
14. For confidentiality reasons, the AHS identifies location in the central city of a large SMSA for only 50 of the 125 large SMSAs.
15. On hedonic pricing techniques and racial discrimination in housing markets see King and Mieszkowski (1973), Kain and Quigley (1975), Olsen (1974), Daniels (1975), and Lapham (1971). On values of different housing characteristics see Gillingham (1975), Goodman (1978), Grether and Mieszkowski (1974), Kain and Quigley (1970), King (1976), Ridker and Henning (1967), and Straszheim (1973). On price indexes see Follain et al. (1979) and Malpezzi et al. (1980). On market rents see Olsen (1972) and Olsen and Barton (1983).
16. Only 4.8 percent of subsidized units in the sample are furnished.
17. Four-room housing units account for 36 percent of the nonwhite sample and 34 percent of the white sample.
18. See Maddala (1977, pp. 174–5) and Kmenta (1971, pp. 461–6) for discussions of the nonlinear least-squares method of estimation. In this study the Gauss–Newton iterative estimation procedure contained in the SAS nonlinear regression package is used (see *SAS User's Guide* 1979).
19. Under the assumption that B_h and B_x are the same for all families, the estimates of these parameters are asymptotically unbiased.
20. See Olsen and Barton (1983, pp. 314–15) for a more detailed discussion of this issue.
21. For all sixteen household types, H_{it} estimated from the sample containing both participating and nonparticipating households is substantially less than H_{it} estimated from the sample of participating households only. Using H_{it} estimated from the latter sample results in a less restrictive constraint on the parameter estimates.
22. Two additional households are deleted because of insufficient computer capability to calculate their benefits.
23. Other studies have also found negative displacement parameters for other goods. See Olsen and Barton (1983, pp. 311–12) and MacRae and Turner (1981, p. 352).

Chapter 5

1. This ignores any cost of participating other than rent paid. Other costs include the transaction and stigma costs of participating in a subsidy program, and they may be substantial. See Moffitt (1983) for an attempt to determine the effect of stigma on participation in the Aid to Families with Dependent Children program.
2. In the absence of administrative costs and government inefficiency, $1,046,

$1,136, and $810 represent the mean cost per subsidized family incurred by taxpayers for all subsidy programs combined, the public housing program, and other government housing subsidy programs, respectively. Given the costs of administering the programs and the fact that all existing estimates suggest the government is an inefficient producer of housing services, the mean cost is undoubtedly much greater. See Smolensky (1968), Olsen (1968), Muth (1973), Olsen and Barton (1983), and Mayo et al. (1980) for estimates of government inefficiency in housing production.

Bibliography

Aaron, Henry J. "Income Taxes and Housing." *American Economic Review* 60 (December 1970): 789–806.
 Shelter and Subsidies: Who Benefits from Federal Housing Policies. Washington, D.C.: The Brookings Institution, 1972.

Aaron, Henry J. and von Furstenberg, George M. "The Inefficiency of Transfers in Kind: The Case of Housing Assistance." *Western Economic Journal* 9 (June 1971): 184–92.

Abbott, Michael and Ashenfelter, Orley. "Labour Supply, Commodity Demand and the Allocation of Time." *Review of Economic Studies* 43 (October 1976): 389–411.

Arrow, Kenneth and Kurz, Mordecai. "Optimal Consumer Allocation Over an Infinite Horizon." *Journal of Economic Theory* 1 (June 1969): 68–91.

Atkinson, A. B., ed. *The Personal Distribution of Income.* London: George Allen and Unwin, 1976.

Ball, Michael J. "Recent Empirical Work on the Determinants of Relative Housing Prices." *Urban Studies* 10 (1973): 213–33.

Barten, Anton P. "Estimating Demand Equations." *Econometrica* 36 (April 1968): 213–50.
 "The Systems of Consumer Demand Functions Approach: A Review." *Econometrica* 45 (January 1977): 23–51.

Barton, David M. and Olsen, Edgar O. "The Benefits and Costs of Public Housing in New York City." Discussion Paper 372-75, Institute for Research on Poverty, University of Wisconsin, 1976.

Becker, Gary S. *Human Capital.* 2nd ed. New York: Columbia University Press, 1975.

Becker, Gary S. and Chiswick, Barry R. "Education and the Distribution of Earnings." *American Economic Review* 56 (May 1966): 358–69.

Bish, R. L. "Public Housing: The Magnitude and Distribution of Direct Benefits and Effects on Housing Consumption." *Journal of Regional Science* 9 (December 1969): 425–38.

Blaug, Mark. "The Empirical Status of Human Capital Theory: A Slightly Jaundiced Survey." *Journal of Economic Literature* 14 (September 1976): 827–55).

126

Blinder, Alan S. *Toward an Economic Theory of Income Distribution.* Cambridge: MIT Press, 1974.

"On Dogmatism in Human Capital Theory." *Journal of Human Resources* 11 (Winter 1976): 8–21.

Brown, A. and Deaton, A. "Models of Consumer Behavior." *The Economic Journal* 82 (December 1972): 1145–236.

Brown, J. A. C. "The Mathematical and Statistical Theory of Income Distribution." In *The Personal Distribution of Incomes*, pp. 72–97. Edited by A. B. Atkinson. London: Allen and Unwin, 1976.

Caniglia, A. S. "Intertemporal Effects, Intertemporal Substitutability, and the Analysis of In-Kind Subsidy Programs." *Public Finance Quarterly* 12 (October 1984): 395–406.

Carliner, Geoffrey. "Income Elasticity of Housing Demand." *Review of Economics and Statistics* 55 (November 1973): 528–32.

Champernowne, D. G. "The Place of Stochastic Models of Income Distribution Amongst Other Models of It." In *Income Distribution and Economic Inequality*, pp. 113–31. Edited by Zvi Griliches. New York: Wiley, 1978.

Chiswick, Barry R. *Income Inequality: Regional Analysis Within a Human Capital Framework.* New York: National Bureau of Economic Research, 1974.

Clemmer, R. "Measuring Welfare Effects of In-Kind Transfers." *Journal of Urban Economics* 15 (January 1984): 46–65.

Council of Economic Advisors. *The Economic Report of the President, January 1979.* Washington, D.C.: U.S. Government Printing Office, 1979.

Daniels, Charles B. "The Influence of Racial Segregation on Housing Prices." *Journal of Urban Economics* 2 (April 1975): 105–22.

Deaton, A. S. "The Analysis of Consumer Demand in the United Kingdom, 1900–1970." *Econometrica* 42 (March 1974): 341–67.

Deaton, A. S. and Muellbauer, John. *Economics and Consumer Behavior.* Cambridge: Cambridge University Press, 1980.

DeLeeuw, Frank. "The Demand for Housing: A Review of Cross-Section Evidence." *Review of Economics and Statistics* 53 (February 1971): 1–10.

DeLeeuw, Frank and Ekanem, Nkanta F. "The Supply of Rental Housing." *American Economic Review* 61 (December 1971): 806–17.

DeLeeuw, Frank and Leaman, S. H. "The Section 23 Leasing Program." In *The Economics of Federal Subsidy Programs. Part 5, Housing Subsidies.* A compendium of papers submitted to the Joint Economic Committee of the Congress of the United States, Washington, D.C.: U.S. Government Printing Office, 1972.

DeSalvo, Joseph S. "Reforming Rent Control in New York City: Analysis of Housing Expenditures and Market Rentals." *Regional Science Association Papers* 27 (1970): 195–227.

"A Methodology for Evaluating Housing Programs." *Journal of Regional Science* 11 (1971a): 173–85.

An Economic Analysis of New York City's Mitchell-Lama Housing Program. New York: New York City Rand Institute, 1971b.

"Neighborhood Upgrading Effects of Middle-Income Housing Projects in New York City." *Journal of Urban Economics* 1 (July 1974): 269–77.

"Benefits and Costs of New York City's Middle-Income Housing Program." *Journal of Political Economy* 83 (August 1975): 791–807.

Diewert, W. E. "Intertemporal Consumer Theory and the Demand for Durables." *Econometrica* 42 (May 1974): 497–517.

Dixon, Peter, Bowles, S., and Kendrick, D. *Notes and Problems in Microeconomic Theory.* New York: North-Holland, 1980.

Elliot, J. W. "Measuring the Expected Real Rate of Interest: An Exploration of Macroeconomic Alternatives." *American Economic Review* 67 (June 1977): 429–44.

Fisher, Irving. *The Theory of Interest.* New York: Kelley and Millman, 1954.

Follain, James R. and Malpezzi, Stephen. *Dissecting Housing Value and Rent: Estimates of Hedonic Indexes for Thirty-Nine Large SMSAs.* Washington, D.C.: The Urban Institute, 1979.

Follain, James R., Ozanne, Larry, with Alburger, V. *Place to Place Indexes of the Price of Housing: Some New Estimates and a Comparative Analysis.* Washington, D.C.: The Urban Institute, 1979.

Frankel, J. A. "Inflation and the Formation of Expectations." *Journal of Monetary Economics* 1 (October 1975): 403–22.

Friedman, Milton. *A Theory of the Consumption Function.* Princeton, N.J.: Princeton University Press, 1957.

"Windfalls, the 'Horizon,' and Related Concepts in the Permanent Income Hypothesis." In *Measurement in Economics: Studies in Mathematical Economics and Econometrics,* pp. 3–28. Edited by Carl F. Christ et al. Stanford: Stanford University Press, 1963.

Garfinkel, Irwin and Haveman, Robert. "Earnings Capacity, Economic Status and Poverty." *Journal of Human Resources* 12 (Winter 1977): 49–70.

Geary, R. C. "A Note on 'A Constant Utility Index of the Cost of Living.' " *Review of Economic Studies* 18 (1950–51): 65–66.

Gibson, William E. "Interest Rates and Inflationary Expectations: New Evidence." *American Economic Review* 62 (December 1972): 854–65.

Gillingham, Robert F. "Place-to-Place Rent Comparisons Using Hedonic Quality Adjustment Techniques." Ph.D. dissertation, University of Pennsylvania, 1973.

"Place to Place Rent Comparisons." *Annals of Economic and Social Measurement* 10 (Winter 1975): 153–73.

Goldfeld, S. M. and Quandt, R. E. "Some Tests for Homoskedasticity." *Journal of the American Statistical Association* 60 (1965): 539–47.

Gomery, J. D. and Smolensky, E. "Efficiency and Equity Effects in Benefits from the Federal Public Housing Program in 1965." In *Benefit-Cost Analyses of Federal Programs.* A compendium of papers submitted to the Subcommittee on Priorities and Economy in Government of the Joint Economic Committee of the Congress of the United States, Washington, D.C., 1973.

Goodman, Allen C. "Hedonic Prices: Price Indices and Housing Markets." *Journal of Urban Economics* 5 (October 1978): 471–84.

Grether, D. M. and Mieszkowski, Peter. "Determinants of Real Estate Values." *Journal of Urban Economics* 1 (April 1974): 127–46.

Grieson, Ronald E. "The Supply of Rental Housing: Comment." *American Economic Review* 63 (June 1973): 433–6.

Griliches, Zvi. "Estimating the Returns to Schooling: Some Econometric Problems." *Econometrica* 45 (January 1977): 1–22.

Griliches, Zvi et al., eds. *Income Distribution and Economic Inequality.* New York: Wiley, 1978.

Hause, John C. "The Theory of Welfare Cost Measurement." *Journal of Political Economy* 83 (December 1975): 1145–82.

Hausman, Jerry A. and Wise, David. "Discontinuous Budget Constraints and Estimation: The Demand for Housing." *Review of Economic Studies* 47 (January 1980): 75–96.

Hechman, J. and Polachek, S. "Empirical Evidence on the Functional Form of the Earnings-Schooling Relationship." *Journal of American Statistical Association* 69 (1974): 350–4.

Heckman, James J. "Sample Selection Bias as a Specification Error." *Econometrica* 47 (January 1979): 153–61.

Henderson, James M. and Quandt, Richard E. *Microeconomic Theory: A Mathematical Approach.* 2nd ed. New York: McGraw-Hill, 1971.

Hicks, John R. "The Four Consumer Surpluses." *Review of Economic Studies* 11 (1943): 31–41.

Value and Capital. 2nd ed. Oxford: Clarendon Press, 1946.

A Revision of Demand Theory. Oxford: Clarendon Press, 1956.

Hirshleifer, Jack. *Price Theory and Applications.* 2nd ed. Englewood Cliffs, N.J.: Prentice-Hall, 1980.

Hu, Sheng Cheng. "Imperfect Capital Markets, Demand for Durables, and the Lifetime Allocation Process." *Econometrica* 48 (April 1980): 577–94.

Johnston, J. *Econometric Methods.* 2nd ed. New York: McGraw-Hill, 1972.

Kain, John F. and Quigley, John M. "Measuring the Value of Housing Quality." *Journal of American Statistical Association* 65 (June 1970): 532–48.

Housing Markets and Racial Discrimination: A Microeconomic Analysis. New York: National Bureau of Economic Research, 1975.

King, A. Thomas. "The Demand for Housing: Integrating the Roles of Journey to Work, Neighborhood Quality, and Prices." In *Household Production and Consumption,* pp. 451–84. Edited by Nestor E. Terleckyj. New York: National Bureau of Economic Research, 1975.

"The Demand for Housing: A Lancastrian Approach." *Southern Economic Journal* 43 (October 1976): 1077–87.

King, A. Thomas and Mieszkowski, Peter. "Racial Discrimination, Segregation, and the Price of Housing." *Journal of Political Economy* 81 (May/June 1973): 590–607.

Klein, L. R. and Rubin, H. "A Constant-Utility Index of the Cost of Living." *Review of Economic Studies* 15 (1947–48): 84–7.

Kmenta, Jan. *Elements of Econometrics*. New York: Macmillan, 1971.

Konijn, H. S. "Regression Analysis in Sample Surveys." *Journal of the American Statistical Association* 57 (September 1962): 590–606.

Kraft, John and Olsen, Edgar O. "The Distribution of Benefits from Public Housing." In *The Distribution of Economic Well-Being*, pp. 51–65. Edited by F. Thomas Juster. Cambridge, Mass.: National Bureau of Economic Research, 1977.

Lahiri, K. "Inflationary Expectations: Their Formation and Interest Rate Effects." *American Economic Review* 66 (March 1976): 124–31.

Lapham, Victoria. "Do Blacks Pay More for Housing?" *Journal of Political Economy* 79 (November/December 1971): 1244–57.

Lee, Tong Hun. "The Stock Demand Elasticities of Non-Farm Housing." *Review of Economics and Statistics* 46 (February 1964): 82–9.

"More on the Stock Demand Elasticities of Non-Farm Housing." *Review of Economics and Statistics* 49 (November 1967): 640–2.

"Housing and Permanent Income: Tests Based on a Three-Year Reinterview Survey." *Review of Economics and Statistics* 50 (November 1968): 480–490.

Lee, Tong Hun and Kong, Chang Min. "Elasticities of Housing Demand." *Southern Economic Journal* 44 (October 1977): 298–305.

Liviatan, Nissan. "Tests of the Permanent-Income Hypothesis Based on a Reinterview Savings Survey." In *Measurement in Economics*, pp. 29–59. Edited by Carl F. Christ, et al. Stanford: Stanford University Press, 1963.

Lydall, Harold F. *The Structure of Earnings*. London: Oxford University Press, 1968.

"Theories of the Distribution of Earnings." In *The Personal Distribution of Income*, pp. 15–46. Edited by A. B. Atkinson. London: Allen and Unwin, 1976.

MacRae, C. Duncan and Turner, Margaret. "Estimating Demand for Owner-Occupied Housing Subject to the Income Tax." *Journal of Urban Economics* 10 (November 1981): 338–56.

Maddala, G. S. *Econometrics*. New York: McGraw-Hill, 1977.

Maisel, Sherman, Burnham, John, and Austin, John. "The Demand for Housing: A Comment." *Review of Economics and Statistics* 53 (November 1971): 410–11.

Malinvaud, E. *Lectures on Microeconomic Theory*. New York: American Elsevier, 1972.

Malkiel, Burton G. and Malkiel, Judith A. "Male–Female Pay Differentials in Professional Employment." *American Economic Review* 63 (September 1973): 693–705.

Malpezzi, Stephen, Ozanne, Larry, and Thibodeau, Thomas. *Characteristic Prices of Housing in Fifty-Nine Metropolitan Areas*. Washington, D.C.: The Urban Institute, 1980.

Mayo, Stephen K. "Theory and Estimation in the Economics of Housing Demand." *Journal of Urban Economics* 10 (July 1981): 95–116.

Mayo, Stephen K., et al. *Housing Expenditures and Quality: Report on Housing Expenditures Under a Percent of Rent Housing Allowance – Part 1.* Cambridge, Mass.: Abt Associates, 1976.

Housing Allowances and Other Rental Housing Assistance Programs – A Comparison Based on the Housing Allowance Demand Experiment, Part 1: Participation, Housing Consumption, Location, and Satisfaction, and Part 2: Costs and Efficiency. Cambridge, Mass.: Abt Associates, 1980.

Miller, H. P. "Lifetime Income and Economic Growth." *American Economic Review* 55 (September 1965): 834–43.

Mincer, Jacob. *Schooling, Experience and Earnings.* New York: National Bureau of Economic Research, 1974.

"Progress in Human Capital Analysis of the Distribution of Earnings." In *The Personal Distribution of Incomes,* pp. 136–92. Edited by A. B. Atkinson. London: Allen and Unwin, 1976.

Mincer, Jacob and Polachek, Solomon. "Family Investments in Human Capital: Earnings of Women." *Journal of Political Economy* 82 (March/April 1974): S76–S108.

"Women's Earnings Reexamined." *Journal of Human Resources* 13 (Winter 1978): 118–34.

Modigliani, Franco and Ando, A. "The Life Cycle Hypothesis of Saving: Aggregate Implications and Test." *American Economic Review* 53 (March 1963): 55–84.

Modigliani, Franco and Brumberg, Richard. "Utility Analysis and the Consumption Function." In *Post Keynesian Economics,* pp. 388–436. Edited by Kenneth K. Kurihara. New Brunswick: Rutgers University Press, 1954.

Moffitt, R. "An Economic Model of Welfare Stigma." *American Economic Review* 73 (December 1983): 1023–35.

Morgan, Jack and Rozenzweig, Mark R. "Wage Discrimination: A Comment." *Journal of Human Resources* 11 (Winter 1976): 3–7.

Morgenstern, Richard D. "Direct and Indirect Effects on Earnings of Schooling and Socio-Economic Background." *Review of Economics and Statistics* 55 (May 1973): 225–33.

Morrall, John F. and Olsen, Edgar O. "The Cost Effectiveness of Leased Public Housing." *Policy Analysis* 6 (Spring 1980): 151–70.

Murray, Michael P. "The Distribution of Tenant Benefits in Public Housing." *Econometrica* 43 (July 1975): 771–88.

"Hedonic Prices and Composite Commodities." *Journal of Urban Economics* 5 (April 1978a): 188–97.

"Methodologies for Estimating Housing Subsidy Benefits." *Public Finance Quarterly* 6 (April 1978b): 161–92.

Muth, Richard F. "The Demand for Non-Farm Housing." In *The Demand for Durable Goods,* pp. 29–96. Edited by Arnold C. Harberger. Chicago: University of Chicago Press, 1960.

Cities and Housing. Chicago: University of Chicago Press, 1969.

Public Housing: An Economic Evaluation. Washington: American Enterprise Institute, 1973.

Nie, Norman H. *SPSS: Statistical Package for the Social Sciences.* 2nd ed. New York: McGraw-Hill, 1975.

Nourse, H. O. "The Effect of Public Housing on Property Values in St. Louis." *Land Economics* 39 (November 1963): 434–41.

"Redistribution of Income from Public Housing." *National Tax Journal* 19 (March 1966): 27–37.

Oaxaca, Ronald. "Sex Discrimination in Wages." In *Discrimination in Labor Markets,* pp. 124–51. Edited by Orley Ashenfelter and Albert Rees. Princeton, N.J.: Princeton University Press, 1973.

Olsen, Edgar O. "A Welfare Economic Evaluation of Public Housing." Ph.D. dissertation, Rice University, 1968.

"A Competitive Theory of the Housing Market." *American Economic Review* 59 (September 1969): 612–22.

"Subsidized Housing in a Competitive Market: Reply." *American Economic Review* 61 (March 1971): 220–5.

"An Econometric Analysis of Rent Control." *Journal of Political Economy* 80 (November/December 1972): 1081–101.

"Do the Poor or the Black Pay More for Housing?" In *Patterns in Racial Discrimination.* Vol. 1: *Housing,* pp. 205–11. Edited by G. M. Von Furstenberg, Bennett Harrison, and Ann R. Horowitz. Lexington, Mass.: Lexington Books, 1974.

"Housing Policy and the Forgotten Taxpayer." *Public Interest* 66 (Winter 1982): 97–109.

Olsen, Edgar O. and N. Agrawal. "Aggregation Bias in the Estimation of the Benefits of Government Programs." Discussion Paper 710-82, Institute for Research on Poverty, University of Wisconsin, 1982.

Olsen, Edgar O. and Barton, David M. "The Benefits and Costs of Public Housing in New York City." Discussion Paper 123, The Thomas Jefferson Center for Political Economy, University of Virginia, 1982.

"The Benefits and Costs of Public Housing in New York City." *Journal of Public Economics* 20 (April 1983): 299–332.

Olsen, Edgar O. and Bierman, H. S. "Selection Bias in the Estimation of Benefits of In-Kind Transfers." Discussion Paper 711-82, Institute for Research on Poverty, University of Wisconsin, 1982.

Olsen, Edgar O. and Caniglia, Alan S. "Aggregation Bias in the Estimation of Benefits of Government Programs." Discussion Paper 111, The Thomas Jefferson Center for Political Economy, University of Virginia, 1981.

Olsen, Edgar O. and Prescott, J. R. "An Analysis of Alternative Measures of Tenant Benefits of Government Housing Programs with Illustrative Calculations from Public Housing." The Rand Corporation, P-4129, November, 1969.

Olsen, Edgar O. and York, Kathy A. "The Effect of Different Measures of Benefit on Estimates of the Distributive Consequences of Government Programs." In *Economic Transfers in the United States,* pp. 177–95. Edited by Marilyn Moon. Chicago: University of Chicago Press, 1984.

Ozanne, Larry and Thibodeau, Thomas. *Constructing a Rent Index from the Annual Housing Survey.* Washington, D.C.: The Urban Institute, 1980.

Phlips, Louis. *Applied Consumption Analysis.* Amsterdam: North-Holland, 1974.

Polinsky, A. Mitchell. "The Demand for Housing: A Study in Specification and Grouping." *Econometrica* 45 (March 1977): 447–61.

Polinsky, A. Mitchell and Ellwood, David T. "An Empirical Reconciliation of Micro and Grouped Estimates of the Demand for Housing." *Review of Economics and Statistics* 61 (May 1979): 199–205.

Pollak, Robert A. "Intertemporal Cost of Living Index." *Annals of Economic and Social Measurement* 4 (Winter 1975): 179–96.

Pollak, Robert A. and Wales, Terence T. "Estimation of Complete Demand Systems from Household Budget Data: The Linear and Quadratic Expenditure Systems." *American Economic Review* 68 (June 1978): 348–59.

"Rental Formation in Federally Supported Public Housing." *Land Economics* 43 (1967): 341–5.

Quigley, John M. "What Have We Learned About Urban Housing Markets?" In *Current Issues in Urban Economics,* pp. 391–429. Edited by Peter Mieszkowski and Mahlon Straszheim. Baltimore: Johns Hopkins University Press, 1979.

Reeder, William J. "The Benefits and Costs of the Section 8 Existing Housing Program." *Journal of Public Economics* 26 (April 1985): 349–77.

Reid, Margaret G. *Housing and Income.* Chicago: University of Chicago Press, 1962.

Reid, William J., Jr. "A Benefit-Cost Study of Leased Public Housing." Paper presented at the meetings of the Southern Economic Association, Washington, D.C., November 1980.

Ridker, Ronald G. and Henning, John A. "The Determinants of Residential Property Values with Special Reference to Air Pollution." *Review of Economics and Statistics* 49 (May 1967): 246–257.

Roistacher, Elizabeth. "Short-Run Housing Responses to Changes in Income." *American Economic Review* 67 (February 1977): 381–6.

Rosen, Sherwin. "Human Capital: A Survey in Empirical Research." In *Research in Labor Economics,* pp. 3–39. Edited by Ronald Ehrenberg. Greenwich: JAI Press, 1977.

Rosenzweig, Mark R. "Nonlinear Earnings Functions, Age and Experience: A Nondogmatic Reply and Some Additional Evidence." *Journal of Human Resources* 11 (Winter 1976): 23–7.

Ross, W. B. "A Proposed Methodology for Comparing Federally Assisted Housing Programs." *American Economic Review* 57 (May 1967): 91–100.

Sahota, Gian Singh. "Theories of Personal Income Distribution." *Journal of Economic Literature* 16 (March 1978): 1–55.

Samuelson, P. A. "Some Implications of Linearity." *Review of Economic Studies* 15 (1947–48): 88–90.

Sandell, Steven H. and Shapiro, David. "The Theory of Human Capital and the Earnings of Women." *Journal of Human Resources* 13 (Winter 1978): 103–17.

SAS User's Guide, 1979 Edition. Cary, N.C.: SAS Institute, Inc., 1979.

Smith, Barton A. "The Supply of Urban Housing." *Quarterly Journal of Economics* 90 (August 1976): 389–405.

Smith, Barton A. and Campbell, J. M., Jr. "Aggregation Bias and the Demand for Housing." *International Economic Review* 19 (June 1978): 495–505.

Smolensky, E. "Public Housing or Income Supplements – The Economics of Housing for the Poor." *Journal of American Institute of Planners* 34 (1968): 94–101.

Stone, J. R. N. "Linear Expenditure Systems and Demand Analysis: An Application to the Pattern of British Demand." *Economic Journal* 64 (September 1954): 511–527.

Straszheim, Mahlon R. "Estimation of the Demand for Urban Housing Services from Household Interview Data." *Review of Economics and Statistics* 55 (February 1973): 1–8.

"Hedonic Estimation of Housing Market Prices: A Further Comment." *Review of Economics and Statistics* 56 (August 1974): 404–6.

An Econometric Analysis of the Urban Housing Market. New York: National Bureau of Economic Research, 1975.

Struyk, Raymond J. *Urban Homeownership.* Lexington, Mass.: Lexington Books, 1976.

Tanzi, Vito. "Inflationary Expectations, Economic Activity, Taxes, and Interest Rates." *American Economic Review* 70 (March 1980): 12–21.

Theil, Henri. *Principles of Econometrics.* New York: Wiley, 1971.

Turnovsky, S. J. "Some Empirical Evidence on the Formation of Price Expectations." *Journal of American Statistical Association* 65 (December 1970): 1441–54.

U. S. Congress. Congressional Budget Office. *Federal Housing Policy: Current Programs and Recurring Issues.* Washington, D.C.: U.S. Government Printing Office, 1978.

U.S. Congress. Congressional Budget Office. *Housing Assistance for Low- and Moderate-Income Families.* Washington, D.C.: U.S. Government Printing Office, 1977.

U.S. Department of Commerce. Bureau of Census. *Current Population Reports: Consumer Income.* Series P-60, No. 117. Washington, D.C.: U.S. Government Printing Office, 1978.

Current Housing Reports. Series H-150-76. "Annual Housing Survey: 1977, Parts A, B, C, D, E, F." Washington, D.C.: U.S. Government Printing Office, 1979a.

Data from the Annual Housing Survey. Data Access Descriptions, DAD No. 43. Washington, D.C.: Bureau of the Census, 1979b.

Statistical Abstract of the U.S.: 1979. Washington, D.C.: U.S. Government Printing Office, 1979c.

Current Housing Reports. Series H-170-77-19. Various SMSAs. "Housing Characteristics for Selected Metropolitan Areas." *Annual Housing Survey: 1977 and 1975.* Washington, D.C.: U.S. Government Printing Office, 1977 and 1980.

U.S. Department of Health, Education, and Welfare. National Center for Health Statistics. *Life Tables: Vital Statistics of the U.S. 1976,* Vol. II, Section 5. Hyattsville, Md.: National Center for Health Statistics, 1978.

U.S. Department of Housing and Urban Development. *Housing in the Seventies: A Report of the National Housing Policy Review Taskforce.* Washington, D.C.: U.S. Government Printing Office, 1974.

1977 Statistical Yearbook. Washington, D.C.: U.S. Government Printing Office, 1978.

Annual Housing Survey, 1977 National File: Technical Documentation. Prepared by Data User Services Division, Bureau of the Census. Washington, D.C.: Bureau of the Census, 1979a.

Housing in America: The Characteristics and Uses of the Annual Housing Survey, by John M. Goering, Annual Housing Survey Study No. 6. Washington, D.C.: U.S. Government Printing Office, 1979b.

U.S. Department of Labor. Bureau of Labor Statistics. *Three Standards of Living for an Urban Family of Four Persons,* Bulletin 1570-5. Washington, D.C.: U.S. Government Printing Office, 1967.

CPI Detailed Reports: Consumer Price Index, U.S. and City Averages. Washington, D.C.: U.S. Government Printing Office, various issues, 1975, 1976.

"Current Labor Statistics: Consumer Prices." *Monthly Labor Review* 100 (May 1977): 95–6.

Handbook of Labor Statistics, 1978, Bulletin 2000. Washington, D.C.: U.S. Government Printing Office, 1979.

Vaughn, Garrett. "Sources of Downward Bias in Estimating the Demand Income Elasticity for Urban Housing." *Journal of Urban Economics* 3 (January 1976): 45–56.

Weicher, John C. "Urban Housing Policy." In *Current Issues in Urban Economics,* pp. 469–508. Edited by Peter Mieszkowski and Mahlon Straszheim. Baltimore: Johns Hopkins University Press, 1979.

Housing: Federal Policies and Programs. Washington, D.C.: American Enterprise Institute for Public Policy Research, 1980.

Welfeld, Irving. "American Housing Policy: Perverse Programs by Prudent People." *Public Interest* 48 (Summer 1977): 128–44.

Welland, Jon D. "Cognitive Abilities, Schooling and Earnings: The Question of Functional Form." *Review of Economics and Statistics* 60 (November 1978): 622–7.

Winger, A. R. "Housing and Income." *Western Economic Journal* 6 (June 1968): 226–32.

Wu, S. Y. "Indebtedness and the Consumer Allocation Over Time." *Metroeconomica* 26 (January–December 1974): 97–108.

Yaari, Menahem. "On the Consumer's Lifetime Allocation Process." *International Economic Review* 5 (September 1964a): 304–17.

"On the Existence of an Optimal Plan in a Continuous-Time Allocation Process." *Econometrica* 32 (October 1964b): 576–590.

Yohe, W. P. and Karnosky, D. S. "Interest Rates and Price Level Changes, 1952–60." Federal Reserve Bank of St. Louis *Review,* 51 (December 1969): 19–36.

Index

aggregation bias, 20–1

Agrawal, N., 21

Annual Housing Survey, 1, 2, 21, 47, 71, 101, 123 n8, 124 n14; data used in study, 10, 97, 120 n8; description of, 10–11, 97; gross rent in, 54–6; prices in, 40, 42, 43–4

Barton, David M., 9, 19–21, 22, 59, 61, 94, 98, 122 n15, 124 n23

Becker, Gary S., 45

benefit of housing subsidy programs (*see also* public housing, low-rent): compared to subsidy in 1977, 73, 104; estimates for intertemporal model, 73, 104, 106; Hicksian price-equivalent measure, description of, 12, 13, 70; Hicksian price-equivalent measure, intertemporal, 9–10, 29–30, 34, 70, 96–7, 100–1; Hicksian price-equivalent measure, single-period, 9, 29, 97; Marshall's consumer surplus measure, 12; subsidy given measure, 12 (*see also* distribution of benefit of housing subsidy programs, intertemporal model)

Bierman, H. S., 20, 63

borrowing and lending, 22, 24, 25, 28, 96, 98, 99

capital markets, 25, 121 n4

cash grants: effects on consumption patterns in 1977, 74–6; effects on future consumption patterns, 76–84; effects on tenant welfare, 73–4, 104, 106–7; in place of housing programs, 34

characteristics of subsidized households, 84

Chiswick, Barry R., 45

Clemmer, R., 94, 121 n2

CES utility function, *see* constant elasticity of substitution utility function

Cobb–Douglas utility function, 15, 17–9, 69, 97, 98; benefit formula derived from, 14; definition of, 13; disadvantages of, 14, 28, 122 n16; parameter estimation, 15, 18

constant elasticity of substitution utility function, 17–9, 28, 98

consumer demand theory: intertemporal, 23–6, 99–100; single-period, 23, 99

consumer surplus (*see also* benefit of housing subsidy programs): Hicksian price-equivalent measure of, 9–10, 28, 70, 96; Marshall's measure of, 12

consumption patterns, intertemporal model: estimated changes for 1977, 71–3, 104, 106; estimated

consumption patterns (*cont.*)
changes for the future, 76–84,
104–5, 107; measurement of,
35–6, 54, 71

DeLeeuw, Frank, 122 n10
demand for housing and nonhousing
goods, intertemporal model, 28,
32, 33–4, 100
DeSalvo, Joseph S., 9, 14, 15, 16,
21, 94, 97, 98, 122 n16
Diewert, W. E., 121 n7, 122 n9, 123
n1
distribution of benefit of housing
subsidy programs, intertemporal
model, 1, 96, 105; compared to
single-period models, 93–4, 98–
9, 105–6; cross tabulations by in-
come controlling for household
size, 84–7, 117–9; regressions of
real benefit on household char-
acteristics, 87–92

Ekanem, Nkanta F., 122 n10
Ellwood, David T., 40, 123 n6
expected income, *see* income, house-
hold expected
expenditure on housing and non-
housing goods, 15, 71, 100;
equations derived from intertem-
poral model, 28, 32, 33–4; linear
expenditure system, 28, 122 n13;
in single-period Stone–Geary
model, 29

Fisher, Irving, 23, 39, 40, 99, 101,
121 n3
Follain, James R., 123 n5, 123 n7

generalized CES utility function, 17–
9, 28, 98
Gillingham, Robert F., 15, 41, 98
Goldfeld, S. M., 59, 103
Grether, D. M., 59
Grieson, Ronald E., 122 n10

Hechman, J., 46
Heckman, James J., 62, 63
hedonic rent technique, 15, 18, 41–2,
54, 103
Henderson, James M., 23, 24
Hicks, John R., 23, 24, 25, 97, 99,
121 n1
Hicksian benefit measure, *see* benefit
of housing subsidy programs
household income, *see* income, house-
hold expected
housing allowance program, 107–8
housing subsidy programs, home-
owner, 2, 120 n2
housing subsidy programs, rental
(*see also* public housing, low-
rent, rent supplement program,
Section 8 existing housing pro-
gram, Section 8 new construc-
tion/substantial rehabilitation
program, Section 236 rental
housing assistance program):
federal, 2–8, 96; state and local,
8 (*see also* Mitchell–Lama hous-
ing program)
human capital theory, 45–6, 47, 102

income generating functions, *see* in-
come, household expected
income, household expected, 34–5,
37; calculation of lifetime ex-
pected income, 52–3, 102; esti-
mated income model, 48–52;
measurement techniques, 44–5;
specification of income generat-
ing functions, 45–8
indirect utility function, 13, 35
interest rate, 24–5, 27, 37, 39–40,
101
intertemporal model, *see* benefit of
housing subsidy programs; con-
sumption patterns, intertemporal
model; demand for housing and
nonhousing goods, intertemporal
model; distribution of benefit of

housing subsidy programs, intertemporal model; expenditure on housing and nonhousing goods; public housing, low-rent
intertemporal utility function, *see* utility function, intertemporal

King, A. Thomas, 59
Kraft, John, 9, 15, 16, 22, 94, 97, 98, 122 n16

leapfrogging, 20
length of life, *see* life expectancy
life expectancy, 37, 101, 123 n2
low-rent public housing, *see* public housing, low-rent

Mayo, Stephen K., 12, 28–9, 45, 122 n18, 123 n6
Mieszkowski, Peter, 59
Mincer, Jacob, 45
Mitchell–Lama housing program, 8–9, 14, 94, 96, 97
Murray, Michael P., 9, 17, 18, 19, 22, 94, 98, 121 n5, 122 n16
Muth, Richard F., 122 n10

National Housing Policy Review Taskforce, 16, 94, 98

Olsen, Edgar O., 9, 12, 15, 16, 18, 19–21, 22, 59, 61, 63, 94, 97, 98, 121 n1, 121 n5, 122 n15, 122 n16

participation in housing program, length of, 38, 101
Phlips, Louis, 23, 26
Polachek, S., 46
Polinsky, A. Mitchell, 40, 123 n6
prices of housing, Bureau of Labor Statistics (*see also* prices of housing, Urban Institute), 15, 18, 21, 40, 98, 101–2, 123 n5; combined with AHS data, 43–4; combined with Urban Institute

prices, 43, 101–2; problems with, 40–1, 102
prices of housing, Urban Institute (*see also* prices of housing, Bureau of Labor Statistics), 40, 41–4, 101–2
prices of nonhousing goods, 15, 18, 40, 98, 101, 123 n5; combined with AHS data, 42–3; problems with, 40–1, 102
public housing, low-rent, 3, 6, 15, 17, 96, 97–8; benefit of, intertemporal model, 73, 94; benefit of, single-period models, 16, 17, 18, 19, 22, 94; distribution of benefit, intertemporal model, 87, 89, 90–2; distribution of benefit, in single-period studies, 16, 18–9, 20, 93–4; effects on consumption patterns, intertemporal model, 71, 94–5; effects on consumption patterns, in single-period studies, 16, 17, 19–20, 22, 94; household characteristics, 84

Quandt, Richard E., 23, 24, 59, 103

real interest rate, *see* interest rate
Reeder, William J., 21
relative prices (*see also* prices of housing, Bureau of Labor Statistics; prices of housing, Urban Institute; and, prices of nonhousing goods), 27, 40–4
rent, market, of subsidized housing, 37, 54; estimation of, ordinary least-squares model, 54–6, 103; estimation of, weighted least-squares model, 59–61; 103; heteroskedasticity, 59, 103; in previous studies, 15, 19, 98
rent, subsidized, 37, 53–4, 103
rent supplement program, 3, 6–7, 17, 96, 98
rent-to-income ratio, 15, 53, 97

saving and dissaving, *see* borrowing and lending

Section 8 existing housing program, 3, 7–8, 21, 96

Section 8 new construction/substantial rehabilitation program, 3, 7, 96

Section 235 homeownership assistance program, 2, 120 n2

Section 236 rental housing assistance program, 3, 6, 17, 94, 96, 98

selection bias, 20–1, 62–3

Smith, Barton A., 122 n10

Stone–Geary utility function, intertemporal, 22, 27, 30–2, 33, 100; advantages of, 28; benefit formula derived from, 34–5; estimation of parameters, 61–2, 63–9, 100, 103; interpretation of parameters, 29

Stone–Geary utility function, single-period, 19, 98

subsistence quantities of housing and nonhousing goods, 29, 68–9, 98

supply of housing, long-run, 26, 122 n10

Tanzi, Vito, 39–40, 101

tenant rent, *see* rent, subsidized

utility function, intertemporal (*see also* Stone–Geary utility function, intertemporal), 9, 22, 24, 25, 99

Vaughn, Garrett, 122 n10

wealth constraint, intertemporal, 24, 25, 27–8, 31–2, 33, 99, 100

Weicher, John C., 2

Welland, Jon D., 46

York, Kathy A., 121 n1, 121 n5